FA
MONEY-...
SP...

A CONSUMER'S GUIDE TO
LUMP-SUM
INVESTMENT

The Daily Telegraph

A Family Money-Go-Round Special

A Consumer's Guide to
Lump-Sum Investment

Diana Wright

Published by Telegraph Publications
Peterborough Court,
At South Quay,
181 Marsh Wall,
London E14 9SR

First edition 1985
Third edition 1986
Fourth edition 1987

© Telegraph Publications 1986

This book is sold subject to the condition that it shall not, by way of trade or otherwise, be lent, re-sold, hired out or otherwise circulated without the publisher's prior consent in any form of binding or cover other than that in which it is published.

All rights reserved. No part of this work may be reproduced or transmitted by any means without permission.

Produced for Telegraph Publications by William Curtis Limited

Typeset by ABM Typographics Limited, Hull
Printed in Great Britain by Biddles Ltd, Guildford, Surrey

British Library Cataloguing in Publication Data

Wright, Diana
   A consumer's guide to lump-sum investment.
   ——New. ed.——(A Family money-go-round special).
   1. Investments——Great Britain
   I. Title II. Series
   322.6′78′0941   HG5435

ISBN 0–86367–184–5

CONTENTS

INTRODUCTION TO THE SERIES ix

ACKNOWLEDGEMENTS xi

AUTHOR'S PREFACE xiii

CHAPTER 1. INTRODUCTION 1

CHAPTER 2. FIXED CAPITAL INVESTMENTS (I): BANKS, BUILDING SOCIETIES, NATIONAL SAVINGS 19
The banks   21
Building societies   24
National Savings   25
Premium Bonds   28
Index-linked certificates   29

CHAPTER 3. FIXED CAPITAL INVESTMENTS (II) 33
Guaranteed income and growth bonds   34
Tax position   36
Certificates of tax deposit   37
Offshore money funds   37

CHAPTER 4. THE GILTS MARKET 41
The background   41
The terms   42
Gilts and tax   44
Payment of interest   45
Gilts and the private investor   46
How to buy and sell gilts   49

CHAPTER 5. EQUITIES 51
The Stock Exchange   51
The private investor   54
What is an ordinary share?   55
Why do share prices move?   56
Dividends and how to judge them   57
Price/earnings ratio   59
How to buy and sell shares   60

The other costs of dealing and when you pay them 62
The UK market and the indices 63
The place of shares in a portfolio 64
Other ways to play the equity market 68
Other types of share 70
The menagerie of the stock market 71
Personal equity plans (PEPs) 72

CHAPTER 6. UNIT TRUSTS AND OFFSHORE FUNDS (I) 75
What is a unit trust? 76
Different types of unit 81
Unit trusts and tax 83
Special facilities for the investor 83
Keeping track of your investment 85
Offshore funds 86

CHAPTER 7. UNIT TRUSTS AND OFFSHORE FUNDS (II): THE INVESTMENT CHOICE 91
Choosing a trust: your investment aim 95
Income 95
A plea for general trusts 98
Growth trusts 99
Offshore funds: the investment choice 102

CHAPTER 8. INVESTMENT TRUSTS 105
The share price – and the discount 105
Investment characteristics of investment trusts 108
How to keep track of prices 109
Variations on a theme 110

CHAPTER 9. LIFE ASSURANCE AND FRIENDLY SOCIETY INVESTMENTS 115
Single premium bonds 115
The tax position 117
Investment considerations 118
Bonds or unit trusts 118
Personalised bonds 119
Broker bonds 119
Annuities 120
Alternatives to the basic annuity 120
'Back to back' income plans 122
Friendly societies 123

CHAPTER 10. PENSION PLANNING   125
Where to find out more   129

CHAPTER 11. TANGIBLES AND OTHER INVESTMENTS   131
Gold   131
Platinum   134
Diamonds   134
Wine   135
Carpets   136
Forestry   136
Theatre productions   136
Business Expansion Schemes   137
Becoming a member of Lloyd's   138

CHAPTER 12. WHERE TO GO FOR PROFESSIONAL ADVICE   141
The merchant banks   143
The stockbroker   144
Accountants   145
Members of FIMBRA   146
Insurance brokers   146
How to choose your adviser   147
How to complain – and when not to   148
Do you need advice?   150

CHAPTER 13: FINANCIAL PLANNING IN PRACTICE: MODEL PORTFOLIOS   151

INDEX   159

WHAT Investment

ONLY WINNERS NEED APPLY

Some people believe that taking part is more fun than actually winning. But now you can have the pleasure of both, with the magazine that puts you on the inside track every time. It's WHAT INVESTMENT, the friendly, informative monthly publication that takes the struggle out of making money. Just look at what you'll receive when you subscribe:—

* Decisive pointers on how to invest your money for the best returns.
* Hot tips from Joe Bloggs, the man in the street with the golden touch.
* Direct access to our exclusive telephone Investment Hotlines with up-to-the-minute news on what shares to buy ... and sell.
* The inside story on a different leading British company every month.
* Advice and recommendations on unit trusts.

Now, you can be a winner and have fun in the process, with WHAT INVESTMENT, the magazine that gives you a complete guide to what's going on in the world of money. ACT NOW ... SUBSCRIBE TODAY!

Name_____

Address_____

_____

_____

Signature_____ Date_____

I enclose a cheque for £22.60 made payable to Financial Magazines Ltd

Please debit my ☐ Access ☐ Visacard ☐ American Express

Card No. ☐☐☐☐☐☐☐☐☐☐☐☐☐☐☐☐

Please complete and return to: WHAT INVESTMENT, Subscription Department, 40-42 Campus Road, Listerhills Science Park, West Yorkshire, BD7 1HR.

WI41

EDITOR'S INTRODUCTION TO THE SERIES

Most of us have so few lump sums that we cannot afford to invest them wrongly. We take care in spending a few hundreds on a holiday to ensure that our enjoyment is not ruined; we take care in spending a few thousands on a car to make sure it will do what we want when we want; and we may spend months debating the merits of one house against another when we have tens of thousands to spend. By the time we take these decisions we are usually thoroughly versed in what to look for, what to ask and what we should pay. Why then treat investment any differently when that investment is in a clearly financial product such as shares or pensions rather than in a holiday or a house?

Perhaps the answer is that financial investments are anything but clear to most people. A mystique has developed around many quite simple investments – no doubt fostered by salesmen eager to exaggerate the claims of their particular product. And while most people positively enjoy asking friends or relatives about makes of car or holiday locations, there is a tendency not to discuss matters so private as our personal finances. It is easy to remain ignorant of what the alternatives are therefore – particularly with decisions whose correctness will not be demonstrated until the long term, as is the case with many lump-sum investments. It thus requires a book which can cut through the complexities and confusions with a clear and concise explanation of the choices available.

Because lump-sum investment is a one-off decision there is not the chance to get matters right next time. If we buy the wrong brand of coffee in the wrong supermarket on one occasion the loss is mere pennies and the mistake can be corrected next time. Investing a lump-sum wrongly can cost thousands of pounds, and even if the lesson is learnt, there may no longer be a lump-sum to invest more wisely. Indeed, even those people lucky enough to have a subsequent sum to invest may not realise how the factors influencing their decision have changed since their first investment. Pensions and shares and unit trusts are constantly changing products in an environment frequently changed by economic or political circumstances.

Some readers of this book may be comforted to know that an investment decision which they have already made, or which was made for them, appears to be sound. They may understand for the first time the exact nature of the investment they have made – and they may decide now that they could afford to be a little more adventurous or would like to invest in something slightly more secure. This book should help them by saying whether they can undo that earlier decision and what choices they have. Other readers may still have their decision to make: for them the book can explain which particular types of investment best suit different people with different objectives and different taxation and other circumstances. And there is no single correct answer for anyone: the book details how a mixture of the different types of lump-sum investments can meet people's different needs.

The personal finance pages of *The Daily Telegraph* appear twice a week and help to answer many of the problems posed by investors. It is the most comprehensive such section to appear in any newspaper and it can keep readers up to date on changes affecting their finances and complement the daily coverage of investment in general. But while such pages can alert readers to the decision they need to make, it requires books such as these to collate all the information and advice into an easily retrievable form. Some people may want to read the book cover-to-cover to explore all the possibilities for investment; others may dip into it to solve particular problems as they arise. This is one of a series of books covering subjects as diverse as air-fares and divorce, but all the volumes have a common aim: they do not attempt to make readers into experts in subjects which they might encounter only occasionally – they provide the advice of experts when it is required. This updated volume, taking account of the changes in the investment world, fits precisely into that pattern.

Richard Northedge
Deputy City Editor
The Daily Telegraph

ACKNOWLEDGEMENTS

Thanks are due to Patrick Whittingdale of Whittingdale Limited for offering advice on Chapter 4, to Christopher Gilchrist of *What Investment* for reading and offering suggestions on Chapters 6 and 7; and to Ray Kelly of stockbrokers James Capel for checking over Chapter 8.

DUNEDIN

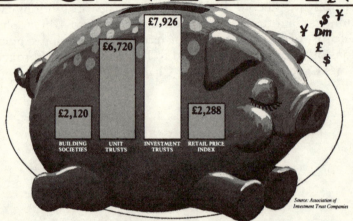

Source: Association of Investment Trust Companies

Lump it and leave it

Hardly the advice you would expect from your financial advisor. But if you had invested a lump sum, say £1,000, and left it in only an average performing investment trust over the last ten years, you can see from the chart how it would have grown – from £1,000 to a massive £7,926* leaving banks and building society deposits well behind. Dunedin now offers to investors a savings plan for buying shares in any of four investment trusts investing in UK and international markets – markets with growth prospects. Either together or separately these trusts aim for capital or income growth or a mixture of both. Special features of the Plan are: **Minimum lump sums £250; minimum monthly savings £30; no initial or 'front-end' fees; low dealing costs; efficient and simple paperwork; professional independent investment management.** For a copy of the Savings Plan booklet including details on each investment trust and application forms please call Colin Peters on 031-225 4571 or just post the coupon.

* Chart shows average growth of £1,000 invested in Investment Trusts in the ten years to end-February 1987, compared with similar returns from unit trusts and building societies. Retail Price Index (on a base of 1,000) also shown over the same period, indicating rate of inflation suffered in that time.

DUNEDIN
FUND MANAGERS LTD
3 Charlotte Square, Edinburgh EH2 4DS
Telephone 031-225 4571

Post to:
Dunedin Fund Managers Ltd
FREEPOST Edinburgh EH2 0BU
or Telephone 031-225 4571
Please send me details of the Dunedin Investment Trust Savings Plan. The booklet contains an application form.

Name_____

Address_____

Telephone_____

LSI 9/87

AUTHOR'S PREFACE

If you have a lump sum, there is no easy answer as to where you ought to invest it, though plenty of answers on where you might: banks, building societies, unit trust groups and life assurance companies are all eager customers for your money. You might choose to invest in gilts, or blue chip equities, or unlisted securities or even gold or diamonds, or the latest theatre production.

For many people, the inheritance of a lump sum (or the gradual accumulation of one) will bring them up against opportunities – and problems – they have never needed to face before.

They can seek expert advice (and again, there is no shortage of possible sources for this – a problem of choice in itself) or decide to undertake the investment decisions themselves. Either way, this Guide is designed to provide the background information and to set out the ground rules for investors to make the best and most appropriate use of their money – and to get the best out of all the advice and information that is available, once they know where to look for it and know how to judge it.

August 1987
Diana Wright

£9,425 profit since February 1983.

HUNDREDS OF PEOPLE HAVE DOUBLED THEIR SAVINGS IN UNDER FOUR YEARS.

Got £5,000 invested somewhere? Has it earned you £9,425 in 53 months? If not, then maybe you should invest it elsewhere. If you'd picked Commercial Union's Prime Life Managed Fund, and put £5,000 into it in February 1983, you would, by July 1987, have shown a profit of 188.5% net of all charges.

And you could have cashed in your holding at any time. Profits are tax free to basic rate tax payers.

The value of units can of course go down as well as up, and past performance is not necessarily a guide to the future.

But at each of its first three anniversaries since its launch in February 1983, it was Britain's most successful Insurance Company Managed Fund and continues to be one of the best, maintaining second position ever since.

If you'd like an opportunity to invest in the Fund through a Prime Investment Bond, and are resident in the UK, all you need is £2,000 or more.

So fill in the coupon now, or phone Allan Ball on 01-681 2929 (Ansaphone service outside business hours). A leaflet with details will be sent to you completely free. It involves no obligation. It doesn't even cost a stamp.

CU Prime Investment Bond.

Feb '84 £1,610 profit
Feb '85 £3,745 profit
Feb '86 £4,860 profit
Feb '87 £7,100 profit

188.5% growth over 53 months since launch.

To: Commercial Union Assurance, FREEPOST, Phoenix Way, Cirencester GL7 1BR. (No stamp needed.) Please send me free and without obligation your leaflet about the CU Prime Investment Bond.

Surname Mr/Mrs/Miss _____
Forenames _____
Address _____
Postcode _____

CU Life is for living.

CHAPTER 1

INTRODUCTION

This book starts off on the cheerful assumption that on the whole money is a good thing. I have also assumed it is worth taking time and effort to preserve it and to increase it – at any rate during some periods of our lives, even if at a later date we are intending to go through a 'spend, spend, spend' phase.

This assumption is accepted probably by the majority of people, which is just as well. If it were not, a consumer's guide to lump sum spending would be infinitely more difficult to write, as it would have to take into account all your varied purposes and pleasures.

All the same, there is an element of that difficulty in an 'Investment' book as well. What use is a chapter on building societies, say, to the individual who sees investment as a game of share spotting? Or what is the point in describing a long term growth strategy (with attendant risks and rewards) to the newly retired couple whose primary aim may simply be preservation of capital while seeking a reasonable income?

There is no such thing as the 'right' investment portfolio in all circumstances, it must depend on several variables:
1 The amount of time you have.
2 The amount of money you have.
3 What you want it to do for you.
4 What your personal attitude to risk is.

Another variable, perhaps less important now than it used to be, but one not to be ignored, is your tax situation.

This book aims to provide background information and possible ways forward for anyone who has upwards of £500 to invest. There has to be an upper limit somewhere but it is difficult to know where to draw it: there is no reason why a millionaire should not find the book almost as relevant as the £500-man. It would be fair to say, though, that the bulk of the book is aimed at people in the middle band with anything between a few thousand and perhaps a hundred thousand pounds to invest.

There are many ways of dividing lump sum investments into categories. The *Oxford English Dictionary* defines 'investment' as 'the employment of money in the purchase of anything from which interest or profit is expected' – which leaves the field pretty open.

One way of categorising lump sum investment would be

purely by the type of vehicles used: insurance bonds, versus unit trusts, versus investment trusts, for example; another way would be the underlying investments involved: shares, gilts and other fixed interest investments, property and so on. Or we could simply look at investments from the point of view of the degree of risk involved, starting off from the rock bottom of security with National Savings Certificates and progressing by degrees up to the airy flights of USM stocks.

The plan this book has adopted is in fact something of a mixture of all three. Chapters 2, 3 and to some extent 4 are about different types of fixed interest investment. The share-spotting fanatic is likely to skip them all – he is welcome to. Most of us, though, are likely to be interested in this class of investment at least to some extent.

These days, everyone knows – as the building societies, in particular, keep on telling us – that we should 'make our money work for us'. Indeed, from reading the pages of the financial press, it sometimes seems that there is no greater sin than leaving cash lying around idle in a current account, doing nothing, earning no interest.

But we all need a cushion of cash to help us through the ups and downs of an average bill-paying life, and this is where building societies come into their own. This is short term 'cash flow management'; but fixed interest investments have a longer term role to play as well. Most people feel happier with at least some of their assets locked away in 'safe' investments. In fact far too many of them, in the opinion of most fund managers, will not venture outside this category.

Here we have to have a go at defining what 'risk' is – and what 'safety' is, come to that. My own (admittedly illogical) feeling is that I am prepared to undergo any degree of risk as long as I am guaranteed a nice fat reward at the end of it. You may laugh: but in fact, this is what people do ask for, time and again. The only investment advice they want is the name of the share that is going to double (treble, quadruple – depending on the size of their ambition) in the next six months.

Tip sheet proprietors make healthy livings out of this. One wonders why people do not stop to think why the tipsters bother running newsletters at all, if the advice is really as good as they claim.

There are two distinct types of risk, as far as investment is concerned – and there is also a certain danger as well. Risk number one is putting all your eggs in one basket – investing in a single share, for example, or putting all your money in a deposit account with some offshore bank. Then if the company goes bust or the bank collapses you have lost everything. And yes, it does happen: remember Rolls Royce, remember the Savings & Investment Bank on the Isle of Man. In a way, this is the least frightening aspect of risk, because it is so easy to do something about. You spread your investments among a number of different shares (for example); or you make sure you choose a reputable bank with some sort of legal investment protection scheme. Then if a company goes into liquidation, it is only a small part of your overall portfolio down the drain; if you have chosen your bank wisely, it simply will not got bust – unless, of course, the entire world banking system goes.

The second risk is something that any investor who steps outside the cosy field of banks or building societies or National Savings has to come to terms with sooner or later. If you invest in something that has the potential for capital growth, by definition it also has the potential for capital *loss*. The stock market is the most obvious home of this type of investment. Figure 1 shows the progress of the FT-Actuaries All Share Index since 1970. The trend, true enough, is generally upwards – but as you can see, there have been plenty of opportunities to lose money along the way as well.

Perhaps the most glaring example is an investor who brought shares at the top of the market at the beginning of 1972. Assuming the shares chosen behaved in line with the index, he would then have had to wait five or six years until he even started to show a profit (and how many people would have panicked and realised a loss instead of sitting tight?).

For all that, the chart is reassuring in one sense: if you do have the time to play with, you can afford to take a 'riskier' (in this second sense) approach to investment. Too many people want to know where they should invest their money 'but only for the next nine months'. In that sort of circumstance, the only sensible answer has to be a building society (or bank, National Savings, etc.). Otherwise, the risk of your losing at least part of your money is too great.

Those are the two risks, then: what about the danger? It is that boring old enemy from a decade ago – inflation. Anybody who experienced the tidal waves of inflation we had through-

Figure 1 London F.T.A. All-Share Price Index
from 1/1/70 to 12/8/87 monthly
Source: *Datastream*

Table 1 Inflation
What £1,000 would be worth (in today's terms) in the future

Years ahead	Annual rate of inflation		
	at 3%	at 5%	at 8%
	£	£	£
1	971	926	926
2	943	907	857
3	915	864	794
4	888	823	735
5	863	784	681
6	837	746	630
7	813	711	583
8	789	677	540
9	766	645	500
10	744	614	463
15	642	481	315
20	554	377	215
25	478	295	146

out the 1970s may well feel that with inflation at 'only' 4 per cent or 5 per cent, it is not something we should be too worried about. Maybe Table 1 will suggest otherwise. At a 5 per cent rate, in 10 years' time your £1,000 of capital will have diminished to a mere £614. After 20 years, it will be down to a miserable £377. Even at 3 per cent, you will have lost about a quarter in real terms over 10 years. And who among us can be confident that inflation will remain as low as 5 per cent in the future? The long term record of inflation, shown in Table 2, does not give that much hope for the future.

Table 2 Average annual inflation rates from 1970 to 1985

	%
1970	+7.8
1971	+9.0
1972	+7.6
1973	+10.6
1974	+19.2
1975	+24.9
1976	+15.1
1977	+12.1
1978	+8.4
1979	+17.2
1980	+15.1
1981	+12.0
1982	+5.4
1983	+5.3
1984	+4.6
1985	+5.7
1986	+3.6

Source: Phillips and Drew.

However you invest your money, there is practically no escape from the effects of inflation: it is not a risk, in other words, but a certainty. The qualification is there because there are now limited means by which you can enjoy a guaranteed return from your investments which is linked to inflation: index-linked gilts (Chapter 4) or index-linked National Savings Certificates (Chapter 2).

In that case, why is there not a rush with investors scurrying to buy these index-linked investments? There is a simple reason for this, you pay dearly for that sort of security. The fourth issue of Index-linked Certificates pays a fixed, tax-free, interest of 4.04 per cent a year for five years in addition to the index-linking. The Government had to introduce this new issue to try to stop investors deserting in droves to more rewarding investments. If you opt for total security, in other words, you are still running the risk of missing out on better opportunities elsewhere.

Somewhere along the line, in talking about investment, the unavoidable question of tax will arise. For all the talk about 'fiscal neutrality' there is still more hot air than cold facts here: the *way* you invest (in other words, the investment vehicles you use) as well as the *type* of investment you make can both have significant impact on the amount of net return you accrue from your investments.

Profits arising from an investment are likely to be taxed in one of two ways: under income tax regulations or capital gains tax rules. Interest or dividends paid are 'income' and you pay tax at your highest income tax rate at the time the income is paid. Capital growth, on the other hand, comes under capital gains tax (CGT) rules and you face tax only when the profits are realised, and then at a maximum rate of 30 per cent. Table 3 summarizes the position for the tax year 1987/8; in subsequent years, the personal allowances will almost certainly rise and there could well be some more tinkering about.

The main distinction between income and capital gains is likely to remain, however: and this is where the tax system gives you a gentle nudge in the direction of 'risk' investments, in other words, those capable of capital growth. There are two major exemptions from CGT which means, for probably the majority of investors, that they need never pay the tax at all.

In the first place, there is an 'indexation allowance' intended to strip out the part of the gain which is due purely to inflation. This provision was first introduced in the March 1982 budget and applies from 5 April 1982. For assets acquired after this date, the base cost of the asset is increased by reference to the Retail Price Index (RPI) from the month of acquisition to the month of disposal and it is only profits made in excess of this which are liable to tax. If the asset was first acquired before then, incidentally, you can use its market value as at 5 April 1982 in order to work out how much indexation you will be allowed to knock off from the total gain.

Secondly, all individuals have an annual exemption from the tax, which is also index-linked: in 1987/8 it stands at £6,600. When you remember that you can offset any realised capital losses you have made in that year, and deduct all your buying expenses from the gain as well, then it is evident that CGT is that rarity among taxes – a lenient one.

All this is not to say that you should always think of the taxation aspect first when you are choosing investments: the

Table 3 Income tax and capital gains tax

1 Rates of income tax 1987/8

Taxable income £	Rate %	Cumulative on top of band £
0–17,900	27	4,833
17,900–20,400	40	5,833
20,401–25,400	45	8,083
25,401–33,300	50	12,033
33,301–41,200	55	16,378
Over 41,200	60	

Main tax allowances

Single person	2,425
Married man	3,795
Additional personal allowance for children	+1,370
Wife's earned income allowance	2,425
Age allowance (age over 65 in year):	
single	2,960
married	4,675
income limit	9,800
Age allowance (age over 80 in year):	
single	3,070
married	4,845
income level	9,800

(Allowance is reduced by £2 for every £3 of income above the limit, subject to a minimum of normal personal allowance.)

Gain	%
First of £6,600	0
Excess over £6,600	30

Major exemptions:
- *Principal private residence
- *Chattels below £3,000 in value
- *National Savings Certificates
- *Betting winnings including the pools and premium bonds
- *Assets gifted to charity
- *Life assurance policies and deferred annuities, provided you are the original owner
- *Decorations for gallantry (unless purchased)
- *Gilts

Note: Indexation allowance: Original expenditure is scaled up in proportion to increase in RPI from date of acquisition (or March 1982 if later).

boot is very much on the other foot. Losses, after all, are very tax efficient, but that is scarcely a reason for choosing an investment! But a top rate taxpayer, for example, would be silly to put all his money in a deposit account, where 60 per cent of his interest is promptly taken away from him.

The last of the 'big three' taxes, inheritance tax, does not, of course, affect an investor or his investments directly, only when he comes to give them away. As with the old capital transfer tax (CTT), (which inheritance tax replaces) gifts made between husband and wife are exempt from the tax, so in some ways the immediate sting of such a tax has been withdrawn. All the same, it only means that tax has been deferred rather than avoided and may still have to be paid when assets make their way down to the next generation.

Inheritance tax was introduced in the March 1986 budget, and differs from CTT in a number of ways, notably by abolishing any tax on 'lifetime' gifts (other than those made within seven years of death) but introducing a new concept of 'gifts with reservation': in other words, gifts where the donor retains some right, or potential right, to enjoy the benefits from the gift.

Table 4 Inheritance tax rates on or after 17 March 1987

Transfers on death

Value £000	Rate %	Total tax to top of band £
0–90	0	0
90–140	30	15,000
140–220	40	47,000
220–330	50	102,000
over 330	60	

Note: Transfers within 7 years of death will be taxed on a portion of their value at the date of the gift using the death rate scale in force at the time of death.

Years between gift and death	% of value charged at death rates
0–3	100
3–4	80
4–5	60
5–6	40
6–7	20

Main exemptions:
1 All transfers between husband and wife.
2 Annual gifts of £3,000 or less.
3 Small gifts to any person of £250 or less.
4 Gifts on marriage: £5,000 by parents;
  £2,500 by grandparents; £1,000 by anyone else.
5 Gifts that form part of 'normal expenditure from income'.

This move outlawed some extremely popular devices used against the old capital transfer tax which inheritance tax has now replaced, and although the nil rate band was raised substantially in the last budget (see table) there will be plenty of not particularly rich people – homeowners in the South East, for example – whose heirs will face a tax bill when they come into their inheritance.

Coming back to the outline of the book, Chapters 2, 3 and (partly) 4 are about fixed interest investment, the 'safety net' of any sensible investment portfolio. Gilt-edged securities, the subject of Chapter 4, are a difficult animal to categorise: if you buy a gilt and hang on to it like grim death until its redemption date, it is a fixed interest/fixed capital investment. It is also possible to deal in gilts and whilst it means that the guarantees are gone, the opportunities to make profits come into their own.

Table 5 Size of the world's stock markets
Market capitalisation, 1986

Country	US$ billion	% of total
United States	2,203	39.0
Japan	1,746	30.0
United Kingdom	440	7.8
West Germany	246	4.3
Canada	166	2.9
France	150	2.7
Italy	141	2.5
Switzerland	132	2.3
Australia	78	1.4
Netherlands	73	1.3
Hong Kong	53	0.9
Sweden	49	0.9
Spain	42	0.7
Belgium	36	0.6
Singapore/Malaysia	33	0.6

Source: *Morgan Stanley*

Chapters 5 to 8 are the meat in the sandwich. Investment inevitably comes back to equities: ordinary shares of companies traded on the world's stock exchanges. Some people, in fact, would deny the term 'investment' to anything else.

One point not touched on so far is the ability for the small investor (as well as the large one) to go world-wide in search of profits. Table 5 shows the relative size of the world's stock markets: and very salutary reading it is to the typically xenophobic British investor (or rather English: the Scots, for example, have always had a more open-minded approach to investment).

No-one is suggesting that the investor should go off round the various stock markets wheeling and dealing on his own behalf. The only practicable way for the average UK-based investor to invest overseas is via a pooled investment vehicle – a unit trust or an investment trust, for example – among whose ranks he should find more than ample choice.

One point to bear in mind when constructing a portfolio is that the principle of 'spread of risk' applies in two ways. First, as we mentioned above, is the basic adage that you do not put all your eggs in one basket. However, you are not going to fare consistently well as an investor if you simply distribute your investments among a number of identical baskets, all of which could possibly be suffering from the same basic design faults, liable to collapse at the same time. Putting all your money in UK engineering shares, for example, is something not so far removed from this.

Table 6 Performance of some major stockmarkets over the last six years

Country	Years 1980 %	1981 %	1982 %	1983 %	1984 %	1985 %	1986 %
United States	+29	−4	+21	+21	+6	+31	+17
Japan	+29	+15	−1	+24	+17	+43	+99
UK	+39	−11	+8	+16	+5	+50	+26
West Germany	−11	−10	+9	+23	−5	+133	+35
Australia	+52	−23	−22	+53	−13	+20	+42
Hong Kong	+71	−16	−42	−2	+45	+50	+54

Source: *Morgan Stanley*
All figures shown in US dollar terms: capital and dividends.

While world stock markets now appear to be moving more in concert with each other, there are still wide variations, as Table 6 shows. Unless you are totally confident that you can predict next year's winner and are prepared to move your money accordingly, there is a lot to be said for building up a long term reasonably wide spread.

The question of what you want from your investment has not yet been touched on. A few people invest with a very specific intention in mind: to pay school fees, for instance, in so many years' time. Apart from this, there are really only two main reasons for investing: to provide yourself with spending money now, or (for you or someone else) to spend in the future.

Chapter 10 is specifically about saving now to spend in the future; although many people think of pensions as something you save for on a regular basis rather than a lump sum. This subject creeps into this book for two reasons. First, the subject is so important and second, it is possible to devote lump sums to the good cause, as well as regular savings – for those with no pension arranged for them by their employer.

Chapter 11 deals with those 'hedges against inflation' dearly beloved in 1970s, though looking somewhat battered at the moment, things like gold and diamonds.

One point to be made, which ought to be obvious except that it is not always followed, is that the 'right' investment portfolio is going to need overhauling from time to time. Firstly, as investment conditions change and maybe new opportunities occur and secondly, as your own needs change.

The first reasons should be treated with some caution: there are few quicker ways of losing money than constantly chopping and changing between different investments. Remember that while it costs nothing to go in and out of different building societies or banks (unless, that is, you get caught by the loss of interest penalties on long term notice accounts) the majority of investments – whether shares, unit trusts, investments bonds, gold or property – all involve some charge to the investor. Beware of 'churning' your portfolio – or allowing anyone else to do it for you.

As far as the second reason is concerned, despite the fact that investors (being human beings) are infinitely various, there is a typical pattern in an investor's life, which is set out below in the different stages.

Stage one: Low but rising income, high outgoings, first beginnings of accumulation of capital.

Stage two: Higher income, outgoings relatively less, possibly higher tax rates and capital to invest (perhaps augmented by inheritance from the older generation). No need for extra income: capital growth required.

Stage three: Lower income again, probably lower outgoings, need to augment income from investments.

These three stages correspond roughly to youth, middle-age and old-age. The major changeover here is between stages two and three when the emphasis on long term capital growth oriented investments is switched over to lower risk income producing investments. Stage three investors are likely to put a higher percentage of their total financial assets in the fixed interest investments described in the early part of the book.

Even if this book were a 12-volume encyclopedia, the one thing it could not tell you is where to invest now. Even a few months' delay between writing and publication can cause investment advice to look quaintly (and embarrassingly) out of date. Once you have decided roughly what you want to achieve, and the degree of risk you are prepared to take, then there are other places to go for advice on precisely where to invest. Who the advisers are, and what you can expect from them, is dealt with in Chapter 12.

The financial services industry has been undergoing a spate of changes recently, which are set to continue for another few months at least.

First, there was the Stock Exchange, which in the autumn of 1986 gathered up its long skirts and jumped through the hoop of the 'Big Bang' which abolished minimum commissions and enabled outside institutions to take majority interests in stockbroking and jobbing firms.

The stock exchange floor has become deserted as the market makers (jobbers in the old days) deal exclusively by screens; the private investor has found, probably not greatly to his surprise, that the abolition of minimum commission scales may have cut costs for the large institutions but increased them (if anything) for him; and the one thing that does seem to have taken people by surprise is the massively increased volumes of stocks being turned over. It has certainly caught stockbroking firms on the hop and the mountain of paperwork building up as a backlog had practically reached crisis proportions by the summer of 1987. Private investors are learning that patience is essential.

On another front, the Financial Services Act, which becomes effective in 1988, has set up a completely new system of self-regulation for the financial services industry, under the direction of the Securities and Investments Board (SIB), an independent body authorised by the government.

Each part of the industry, from stockbrokers to merchant

banks to the high-street life assurance broker, will have to belong to its appropriate self-regulatory organisation. These organisations – there are five, representing different parts of the industry – work under SIB. For the record, this famous five are: TSA (The Securities Association, representing largely members of the stock exchange) AFBD (The Association of Futures Brokers and Dealers), IMRO (Investment Managers Regulatory Organisation) LAUTRO (Life Assurance and Unit Trust Regulatory Organisation) and FIMBRA (Financial Intermediaries, Managers and Brokers Regulatory Association).

Each will have its own rule book, approved by the SIB, and from January 1988 it will be a criminal offence for any firm to carry on a business that would fall into one of these spheres if it is not a member of the appropriate SRO, or authorised directly by SIB.

In theory – and probably in practice – this new system should cut down on instances of fraud. But investors should always remember that no system is perfect, and there's very little any organisation can do, no matter how well intentioned, to abolish the deliberate fraudster. Meanwhile, and of more practical use, the SIB will set up an industry-wide compensation scheme, which should, again, be running some time in 1988.

Just to round off the pack of initials, firms of solicitors and accountants can also advise on financial matters, and they will not necessarily have to join a self regulatory organisation, if the financial part of their business is only incidental to their mainstream business.

The Law Society and the various accountants' institutes are RPB's – Recognised Professional Bodies – and these can do double duty as a sort of self regulatory organisation.

One of the consequences of the new act is a principle called 'polarisation'. In the past, the line between an independent financial adviser and a life assurance salesman could be a blurred one. Some individuals held themselves out as 'independent' whereas in reality they largely sold one company's products, with perhaps one or two others thrown in to give the appearance of independence.

In future, this will no longer be possible, and advisers must be 'polarised' – either full-time representatives of one company alone, or completely independent. And if they are inde-

GUINNESS FLIGHT
GLOBAL STRATEGY FUND LIMITED

INVESTMENT COVERAGE

Money Funds

U.S. Dollar Money Fund
Sterling Money Fund
Yen Money Fund
Deutschemark Money Fund

Managed Currency Fund

Fixed Interest Funds

Global Fixed Interest Fund
Global High Income Bond Fund
U.S. Dollar Fixed Interest Fund
Sterling Fixed Interest Fund
Sterling Index-Linked Gilt Fund
Yen Fixed Interest Fund
European Fixed Interest Fund

Global Convertible Fund

Equity Funds

Global Equity Fund
North American Fund
U.K. Fund
Japan and Pacific Fund
European Fund
Global Energy Fund
Global Leisure Fund
Global Technology Fund

GUINNESS FLIGHT
FUND MANAGERS (GUERNSEY) LIMITED

P.O. Box 188, La Vieille Cour, St. Peter Port, Guernsey, Channel Islands.
Telephone (0481) 712176 Telex 4191284 GFFUND G

GUINNESS FLIGHT

pendent, there are two cardinal rules they must follow, briefly summarised as 'know your customer' and 'best advice'. In other words, they must be sure that whatever they recommend is suitable for their client, which means knowing the full background of his or her financial situation. And then, they must choose the most appropriate product(s), from the whole range of those available.

'Best advice' does *not* mean advisers have to pick the unit trust which is going to perform best in the future, sad to say! But it does mean they should have extremely good reasons for choosing the products they do recommend, which they may have to explain to their regulatory organisation if asked. Company representatives, too, must follow the rule of 'know your client' and must also give 'best advice' although in this case, of course, it's a very much watered down version, as it is restricted to their company's range of products.

Polarisation was meant to be a help to the customer, so that he would not be misled into thinking he was getting independent advice when he was not. In practice, it's thrown up some bizarre consequences. Some of the clearing banks have decided to split themselves into two: the bank branches will have 'company representative status', meaning that they can offer advice only on their in-house products, while a separate subsidiary company *will* offer independent advice. Of the 'big four' banks, only the National Westminster has opted to become independent. Some of the smaller and regional banks have not yet decided which way to jump.

Some of the building societies, too, are dithering. Since the Building Societies Act 1986, societies have been able to get into fresh fields, such as estate agency and financial advice. Many, of course, have advised on endowment mortgages for some time, but now they will be getting into pensions and other products in a big way.

There is thus no shortage of people willing to dish out advice and eager to sell you products; and in future there will be a host of bodies to complain to if things go wrong (see Chapter 12).

At the end of each chapter, sources of further information and reading are suggested. In fact, it is not shortage of information which is necessarily the problem, but knowing where to get it – or even one stage further back than that, knowing what it is you need to find out! Once you have got the right questions to ask, you are half way to getting the right answers.

Table 7 Long term growth records

1 Equities, net income reinvested

	Annual real return (after inflation) with net income reinvested* %
1918 to 1986	3.0%
1936 to 1986	0.2%
1956 to 1986	2.6%
1966 to 1986	2.3%
1976 to 1986	10.5%
1981 to 1986	17.2%

*After maximum rate of personal tax

2 Equities, gross income reinvested

	Annual real return (after inflation) with gross income reinvested
1918 to 1986	7.3%
1936 to 1986	4.7%
1956 to 1986	7.2%
1966 to 1986	6.9%
1976 to 1986	15.1%
1981 to 1986	20.9%

3 Gilts, gross income reinvested

	Annual real return (after inflation) with gross income reinvested
1918 to 1986	0.9%
1936 to 1986	−1.6%
1956 to 1986	0.0%
1966 to 1986	0.0%
1976 to 1986	6.0%
1981 to 1986	12.6%

Source: *Barclays de Zoete Wedd*.

Even if you have no inclination to construct your own portfolio, it is still worth taking an active interest in what your adviser suggests. Unless you want a really massive construction job done, including various complicated tax matters, you will find that most classes of professional adviser will give at least their initial suggestions to you free of charge. There is nothing to stop you 'shopping around' a few advisers first and comparing their suggestions. Never be reluctant to question their reasons for the advice they give, or to put forward ideas of your own; and always be (slightly) suspicious if someone tells you it is a certainty – as opposed to a reasonable probability – that the market, or the shares of XYZ Company are guaranteed to leap up in the next two weeks.

'The lump sum investor' is not, of course, a completely different character from the 'regular saver', 'the house buyer', 'the family man' and so on: as likely as not, they are all one and the same. Although this book is concerned with lump sum investment, it should go without saying that financial planning is as much to do with making sure you have got sufficient life assurance protection, that you have chosen the appropriate mortgage for your circumstances (and so on and so forth), as it is about disposing of whatever capital you might have in a sensible manner.

Finally, what sort of rewards can you expect from being a model lump sum investor? It all depends, of course, on what happens in the future and perhaps how lucky you are as well! It is interesting, though, to look back and see how well people have done in the past. Table 7 provides a few statistics – and they could make surprising reading to some. Apart from the last few years, when things have undoubtedly been extra bright for investors, the long term growth records might seem fairly low. It is a salutary lesson, really, and one that is probably worth learning: unless you are really prepared to chance your arm and/or risk your shirt, you should forget about 'get rich quick' schemes and concentrate on getting rich slowly!

THE GUINNESS MAHON INVESTMENT OPPORTUNITY PORTFOLIO

European Growth Trust
North American Trust
High Income Trust
Recovery Trust
Global Growth Trust
Pacific Growth Trust

For further information
telephone 01-623 9333 and ask for Jon Broom

**Guinness Mahon
Unit Trust Managers Limited**
32 St Mary at Hill, London EC3P 3AJ Telephone: 01-623 9333

CHAPTER 2

FIXED CAPITAL INVESTMENTS (I): BANKS, BUILDING SOCIETIES, NATIONAL SAVINGS

To start off, we will look at 'fixed capital' investments: those where you can be sure of receiving back £100 capital for every £100 you put in. This makes them ideal for very short-term investments and for the ultra cautious, to whom preservation of the monetary value of their capital is their main or only concern.

With the exception of some of the National Savings products (the Government being able to make its own rules) the rewards arising from this type of investment are interest and are therefore taxed at income tax rates. This makes them good (in general) for basic rate taxpayers and non-taxpayers (but see below, 'Composite Rate Tax', CRT) but of less value the higher up the tax rates you go.

DEDUCTION OF COMPOSITE RATE TAX AT SOURCE

Practically the only organisation in this country that can pay interest gross is the Government. Banks and building societies are forced to deduct basic rate tax at source before handing over the interest to their customers. This is a raw deal for non-taxpayers as the basic rate tax paid on their behalf cannot be reclaimed – but there is nothing they can do about it, other than take their money and run over to National Savings or out of the country.

The composite rate is set once a year by the Inland Revenue. Until now, they have done it by collecting sample statistics from the building societies on how many of their savers are non-taxpayers. The more of them there are, the lower the composite rate will be. In fact, the general trend has been for the composite rate to rise: in the tax year 1979/80 it was set at 21 per cent (with basic rate at 30 per cent); in 1987, the rate is 24.75 per cent with basic rate set at 27 per cent; roughly 91 per cent of the basic rate compared with only 70 per cent five years earlier.

CRT is convenient and marginally advantageous to the basic rate taxpayer: for the higher rate taxpayer, though, the advantage partly evaporates as the interest is 'grossed up' before higher rate tax is imposed. So, for example, if a building society is paying 7 per cent net, the higher rate taxpayer is assumed to be receiving 9.59 per cent gross (not the 9.30 per cent it would actually work out at) and it is on that basis that tax is assessed. Table 8 below shows how the effective rate rises depending on your marginal rate of tax.

Table 8

Marginal rate of tax %	Net of CRT %
27	24.75
40	38.14
50	48.45
60	58.78

FIXED VERSUS VARIABLE INTEREST

As mentioned, the investments dealt with in this chapter are fixed capital. However, the majority of them pay variable interest which moves up and down in line with interest rates generally. On past records, the banks are usually quickest off the mark in altering their interest rates on their various savings accounts; as soon as their base rate moves, all their other rates move along with it.

Building societies have tended to be slower, though in the last year or so, helped by the increasing competitiveness brought about by the break up of their cartel, they seem to have speeded up. National Savings rates generally follow the market but sometimes with a greater time lag, occasionally mixed in with some other dictat of Government policy, for example, the need to meet their savings targets.

It is very much swings and roundabouts whether you win or lose by investing in a 'fast mover' or not, and should not be a factor in deciding where to invest. Of more importance, though, is whether you go for fixed or variable interest. Products such as National Savings Certificates, gilts held to redemption and Guaranteed Income Bonds (Chapter 3) provide a fixed interest rate for a predetermined term, whatever happens to interest rates in the meantime. If they go down, you win: if they rise, you lose.

Forecasting the movement in interest rates over the next

(say) five years is probably somewhat easier than picking the Grand National winner, but not much. One stockbroker, who kept being asked by his clients what was going to happen to interest rates, was reputed to have told those with surnames beginning A to M that they were going up, and the N to Z contingent that they were going down. 'That way', he observed, 'at least I keep half of my clients happy even if I don't know which half'.

If you are in a situation where you need certainty from your investments above anything else, then fixed interest rates have their attractions: and there certainly are times when these products look especially inviting.

THE BANKS

Coming on now to particular products produced by these organisations, we might as well begin right at the beginning.

The current account
A current account does not (usually) pay any interest, indeed it can cost you money to run one; therefore it is not a place for investment money. Over 60 per cent of the population has a bank current account, and given the success the building societies have had of reaching the 'unbanked', the number of people living on a purely cash basis these days is tiny.

To minimise your bank charges cut down as far as possible on the non-automated transactions of cheques and standing orders. Play your cards right: use cash machines for withdrawing cash rather than cheques, use your credit card for shop purchases as that way you can settle several different items with a single cheque to the credit card company. Of course, this latter ploy only works if you manage to settle your credit card bill in one go. If not, you will be paying their rates of around 26 per cent (APR) a year, making it an extremely expensive way of saving money!

According to the latest statistics, 75 per cent of us stick with the same bank for life – which probably explains why all the banks are offering such winning combinations of free magazines, geometry sets, calculators, book tokens and so on to students and the under-16s. Adults, sad to say, are not offered any of these incentives. There is only one theoretical advantage to staying with any bank, which is that you are more likely to be looked on favourably for a loan by your bank manager if you have built up a long, happy relationship with him.

Of course, the banks 'would say that, wouldn't they?' One or two changes in a long banking career are probably neither here nor there; it is the person who changes accounts every few months who would – naturally – be looked upon with suspicion. The reason most people stay with their banks is probably lethargy rather than anything else and the fact that, until recently at any rate, no one offered anything that was much better (or much worse) than anyone else.

But that is beginning to change. The banks' bread and butter business of money transmission is being nibbled at from two sides: by the merchant banks and licensed deposit-takers, and by the building societies.

Money funds and high interest cheque accounts
There are now some 14 variations on this theme, offered by various licensed deposit-takers and merchant banks, and some of the clearing banks have got into the act as well. Some are simply deposit funds, others offer money transmission facilities as well.

The disadvantage with the majority of these funds is that they require high initial deposits – £2,500 is typical, a few stipulate £1,000 or less. The money transmission facilities are in many cases limited. Cheques can generally be written for amounts only in excess of £250. Most of them can therefore only be run in tandem with an ordinary current account, but one or two of the 'market leaders' here have put together a package which is as good as a current account on the facilities side, offering unlimited cheques of any amount, a cheque guarantee card, overdraft facilities, standing orders and so on, plus the big bonus of interest on credit balances.

Increasing competition in this field should ensure that any new developments are all for the better: it has to be a case of 'watch this space!' Whatever improvements are made, however, they are likely to remain the province of the big spender, or rather, the big earner, who has a thousand or more regularly flowing through his account. Clubs, churches and charities will also find them useful.

Deposit accounts

The basic savings fare offered by the banks is their deposit account. There is no minimum investment required, withdrawals are generally at seven days' notice with immediate withdrawals usually allowed with the loss of seven days' interest. Table 9 shows the rates available from Lloyds Bank at time of writing.

Table 9 Bank deposit rates

Account	Notice period	Net interest rate %
1 Variable interest		
Deposit account	none	3.0
Extra Interest: up to £1,000	1 month	3.0
£1,000 to £4,999	1 month	6.0
£5,000 to £9,999	1 month	6.2
£10,000 to £49,999	1 month	6.5
£50,000+	1 month	7.0
Three month account		
£5,000 to £9,999	3 months	6.9
£10,000 to £49,999	3 months	7.2
£50,000+		7.5
2 Fixed rate		
£2,500 to £24,999	1 month	5.5
	3 months	5.125
	6 months	6.625
	12 months	7.0

Note: rates applicable on 6 August 1987. Rates net of basic rate tax.
Bank base rate: 9.0%
Source: *Lloyds Bank*

High interest accounts

All the major banks now have some version of a 'high interest' account, going under various brand names. The minimum investment here is usually £2,000 or £2,500; some of them also have limited cheque book facilities while others are straight deposit accounts. If this type of investment appeals check out the competition offered by the other money funds (see above) but do not go by the interest rate differentials: these will tend to be very small, and the pecking order among them changes fairly frequently.

Term deposit accounts

For larger sums of money (minimum £2,500 plus) fixed rate

term deposits are available. The rates here depend on the amount and the term. They can change daily, closely reflecting money market rates, but once you are locked in at a particular rate, that is what you get for the term.

Offshore bank accounts
Non-taxpayers or others who are determined to receive their interest gross can open deposit accounts offshore. The clearing banks all run equivalents of their 'high interest' accounts from the Channel Islands or Isle of Man where the interest will be paid gross (though liable to income tax in the normal way). Your local branch will give details and arrange to open the account.

BUILDING SOCIETIES

With 25 million of us (at the last count) wielding some 33 million accounts between us, building societies scarcely need any introduction. Societies these days talk grandly of their 'portfolio of savings accounts' and in total the number of different accounts on offer must be over the 1,000 mark. For all their apparent differences, however, all building society accounts are different permutations of just four ingredients:
– the interest rate offered;
– the minimum investment;
– the notice of withdrawal required;
– the penalties (if any) for early encashment.

The two accounts at the bottom of the interest rate ladder are the 'Deposit Account' and the 'Share Account'. Deposit accounts are scarcely ever heard of these days. They pay less than the ordinary share account (by 0.5 per cent or so); their unique selling point is that they are theoretically safer than any other building society investment: depositors are not shareholders, and if the society were to collapse, the deposit account holders would get their money back first, in preference to investors in all the other share accounts.

The main users of such accounts these days are saving clubs and solicitors, who may have to obey extremely strict dictates as to where they can invest money they are holding on others' behalf. The excellent record that societies have enjoyed as regards financial stability and the investment protection scheme that they run mean that the deposit account has become something of a historical oddity. Whether this will always be the case is another matter, as the new legislation on the horizon appears to mean a diminishing in the protection offered. See the section on 'safety' at the end of this chapter.

As regards Ordinary Share accounts – no notice, no minimum investment required – bargains are often to be had among the small societies. At the time of writing, it is societies such as the Hendon, Bedford, Peckham and Cardiff, – hardly, with the best will in the world, household names – who tend to offer the highest rates. The 'immediate access' aspect of ordinary share accounts is, of course, somewhat watered down if you choose a society based hundreds of miles from you with no branches.

The typical 'portfolio' of savings account offered by societies consists of an ordinary share account, a 'Tiered Rate' Instant Access Account which generally requires a minimum investment of at least £500, and will pay a top rate on sums of £10,000 or more, and a 'Three Month Notice Account'. Thereafter, there are all sorts of offerings: 'Six Month Notice Share Account', 'Two Year Term Share Account', 'Regular Savings Accounts' and so on. One point to watch out for is how frequently interest is credited to the account. Some credit their interest half yearly; others have interest credited only once a year. The difference is not enormous: an account that said it paid 9 per cent would in fact only be paying 9 per cent if interest were credited once a year; if credited twice a year, the annual rate works out at 9.2 per cent and if credited monthly, the annual rate is 9.38 per cent. All building societies are now obliged to quote their rate on a common basis known as the 'Compounded Annual Rate' (CAR) which takes into account the frequency with which interest is credited.

NATIONAL SAVINGS

National Savings products divide into three categories: those that pay a variable rate of interest gross; those that pay a fixed rate of interest free of tax; and a couple of oddities: Premium Bonds and index-linked certificates and bonds.

Interest paid gross: income bonds and deposit bonds
Income Bonds at present require a minimum investment of

£2,000 (maximum: £50,000). Interest is paid out on the 5th of each month; the current interest rate is 10.5 per cent a year. This, they say, 'will be varied from time to time (with six weeks' notice) but it will be kept competitive'. On past experience, they seem to keep the interest rate much in line with what building societies pay on their high interest accounts (after allowing for the effect of tax).

Deposit Bonds require a minimum investment of £100 (maximum £50,000). Interest at 10.5 per cent is credited once a year and as with income bonds, is variable. Repayment (in part or full) requires three months' notice.

National Savings Bank investment account
No minimum deposit is required here: at any rate, as long as it is £5 or more. Interest, currently 10 per cent gross, is credited yearly. Withdrawals are at one month's notice.

National Savings Bank ordinary accounts
The Ordinary Account pays interest gross – at the grand rate of 3 per cent if you open the account during the calendar year – but the first £70 worth of interest in any year is free of tax. Husbands and wives each have the £70 allowance. For 60 per cent taxpayers, this is equivalent to 7.5 per cent interest gross, making it just about worth considering; for anyone else, it is a non-starter, though it has limited banking facilities (bill paying, standing orders) which mean it could be useful for non-bank users. If the account is open for the whole of 1987, then interest is payable at the rate of 6 per cent a year, for each calendar month in which the account is credited with more than £500.

INTEREST FREE OF TAX

National Savings Certificates
The latest breeds of National Savings Certificates have followed similar lines: they last for five years, and the minimum investment is usually £25. Each unit grows at a predetermined rate over the five years and although it is possible to cash the units in at any time, the system works to discourage your doing so as the yield increases each year. Table 10 shows how this works for the 33rd issue which is in force at time of writing.

Table 10 National Savings Certificates 33rd issue.

Years after purchase	Value at end of year £	% yield for year	Compound yield % *p.a.
1	26.44	5.76	5.5
2	28.20	6.66	5.75
3	30.40	7.80	6.0
4	33.12	8.95	6.5
5	36.48	10.14	7.0

*Tax free for all tax rates.

Table 11 National Savings Certificates: Should you cash old issues in?

Number	On sale from/to	During year	Yield for year %	When to cash in*
24th	19.4.82–4.11.82	4	9.80	3 months
		5	11.0†	
		thereafter	CER**	
25th	17.11.82–13.8.83	3	7.23	3 months
		4	8.20	
		5	9.65	
26th	15.8.83–19.3.84	3	8.17	3 months
		4	9.37	
		5	10.59	
27th	5.4.84–7.8.84	2	6.23	3 months
		3	7.15	
		4	8.28	
		5	9.37	
28th	8.8.84–11.9.84	2	7.66	3 months
		3	8.93	
		4	10.25	
		5	11.73	
29th	15.10.84–12.2.85	2	6.94	3 months
		3	7.90	
		4	9.03	
		5	10.20	
30th	13.2.85–9.9.85	1	6.76	3 months
		2	7.49	
		3	8.64	
		4	10.01	
		5	11.43	
31st	27.9.85–11.11.86	1	5.76	3 months
		2	6.66	
		3	7.80	
		4	8.95	
		5	10.14	

* Except for the first year in a Certificate's life (during which no increments are added), the repayment value increases for each completed number of months shown above. You should therefore time your encashment accordingly.
** The Common Extension Rate is variable, currently 7.02 per cent.

The maximum investment in certificates varies according to the particular issue. The 33rd issue has a maximum investment of only £1,000, though you can put in an additional £4,000 if this comes from the proceeds of earlier National Savings Certificates. People who want to lock away more money in tax-free investments should also consider the 'National Savings Yearly Plan', a regular savings contract lasting for five years in total, requiring regular payments into the plan for the first twelve months. Minimum is £20 a month; maximum £200 month.

If you have certificates from previous issues locked away, however, you should think twice before cashing them in. Table 12 shows the relevant interest rate you could be earning on certificates from some of the old issues, depending on when you bought them. From the 7th issue onwards, once the certificate has reached the end of its fixed period, it automatically goes on to the 'Common Extension Rate' of interest, currently 7.02 per cent tax-free. If you have already used up your allocation in the current issue they could be worth holding on to.

Earlier issues present a horrendously complicated picture. A couple of leaflets are available from post offices reference numbers NS455 and DNS555/87/03 which give all the relevant information. If you have any certificates from the 1st to 6th issues (which were on sale between 1916 and 1939) get rid of them immediately: they are earning you a maximum of 2 per cent a year! To decide whether to hold on to or to sell the 7th to 16th issues depends upon precisely when you bought them. For example, if you have some of the ninth issue, which was on sale from February 1951 to July 1956, the odds are you will be getting a good rate of interest. In their 31st year, you will earn 8 per cent interest on them (tax free), in their 32nd year, 9.81 per cent, and 9.95 per cent in their 33rd year. So if you bought them in 1954, don't cash them in during 1987!

At the end of their 33rd year, incidentally, these certificates go on to the Common Extension Rate (7.02 per cent) which for basic rate taxpayers at any rate, is not so attractive as an extra interest account at a building society.

PREMIUM BONDS

Premium Bonds are not an investment, of course, they are a

gamble. Each unit costs £1 but the minimum purchase is £10. Inveterate gamblers may accumulate up to £10,000 worth. The prize fund is equivalent to interest of 7.0 per cent, making it a cheap way for the Government to borrow money off us. Bonds have to be held for three clear months before they become eligible for the prize draw. Winnings are free of tax. ERNIE is genuinely impartial and sending him bribes or presents (he has received among other things, a bottle of castor oil, 'to get him moving') has no effect whatsoever.

INDEX-LINKED CERTIFICATES

The 4th index-linked issue is available to anyone, unlike the first issue of 'Granny Bonds' which was only available to those of retirement age. Minimum investment is £25, maximum holding is £5,000. The repayment value of the certificates is linked to the changes in the RPI (the Government, along with the rest of us, assumes that prices will always continue to move up, not down!) and each month the Department for National Savings produces a table showing how much the certificates are worth, depending on the month bought. This is usually reproduced in the financial pages of newspapers.

The certificates pay guaranteed extra interest each year (in addition to the index-linking). The interest, which is tax-free, averages out at 4.04 per cent compound over the five years of the certificate's life. Table 13 summarises all the various conditions applying to the different National Savings products.

SAFETY

All the investments discussed in this chapter are 'safe' in the sense that the capital value will not go down. But what sort of legal protection does the investor have if the organisation he is investing with were to fail? For the record, the position is as follows.

Banks and deposit takers
Under the 1987 Banking Act, individuals' deposits of up to £20,000 will be protected as to 75 per cent.

Building Societies
Savings with Building Societies are protected as to 90% of the first £20,000 with any one society.
National Savings: Guaranteed by the Government: no other protection necessary (or possible!).

Table 12: National Savings Guide

National Savings investment	Maximum holding or limit of deposit	Who may purchase or invest	Income fixed or variable
National Savings Certificates 33rd issue	£1,000 (40 £25 units), may be held in addition to previous issues	Individuals (or jointly), trusts, charities, or societies including registered friendly societies	Fixed for initial term; variable extension rate
National Savings Certificates 4th index-linked issue	£5,000 (200 £25 units); may be held in addition to previous issues	Individuals (or jointly), trusts, charities, or societies including registered friendly societies	Repayment value linked to changes in RPI plus fixed annual supplement (variable after five years)
National Savings Income Bond	£100,000, (£1,000 units), minimum holding £2,000	Individuals (or jointly), children, trusts, charities, clubs, friendly societies and registered companies or other corporate bodies	Variable, paid monthly
National Savings Deposit Bond	£100,000 in £50 units £100 minimum	(same as for Income Bond)	Variable; credited annually
National Savings Bank Ordinary Accounts	£10,000 Minimum £1	Individuals (also jointly), trusts and voluntary bodies	Fixed rates guaranteed for calendar year (rates depend on balance in account)
National Savings Investment Accounts	£50,000 minimum £5	Individuals, (also jointly), trusts, charities, registered companies and other corporate bodies	Variable
Premium Bonds	£10,000, Minimum purchase of 10 £1 units; sold in multiples of 5 units	Individuals over 16 years of age. For children under 16, bonds may be bought by parents, guardians or grandparents	Prizes, not interest
National Savings Yearly Plan	Minimum £20, maximum £200 per month	Individuals	Fixed for initial term; variable extension rate

FIXED CAPITAL INVESTMENTS (I)

Tax position	Notice of withdrawal	How to Buy/Sell
Free of UK income tax and CGT	At least 8 clear working days	*Buy:* through post offices and banks *Sell:* repayment form available through post offices and banks
Free of UK income tax and CGT	At least 8 clear working days	*Buy:* through post offices and banks *Sell:* as above
Interest is taxable but paid in full without deduction of tax at source	3 months. After first year, interest paid in full if 3 months notice given	*Buy:* application form (available from post offices) to be sent with cheque to Bonds & Stock Office *Sell:* repayment forms from post offices
Interest is taxable but credited in full without deduction of tax at source	3 months, after first year, interest paid in full if 3 months notice given	*Buy:* at post offices *Sell:* repayment form available at post offices, to be sent to Deposit Bond Office
First £70 (£140 joint) of annual interest free of UK income tax	Up to £100 on demand. For larger amounts, a few days' written notice	*Buy:* opened at post offices. *Sell:* withdrawals from post offices
Interest is taxable but paid in full without deduction of tax at source	1 month's written notice	*Buy:* opened at post offices (individuals) or via National Savings Bank Glasgow (clubs etc.) *Sell:* withdrawal forms available from post offices
Prizes are free of UK income tax and CGT	At least 8 clear working days	*Buy:* through post offices and banks *Sell:* repayment forms available from post office, to be sent to Bonds & Stock Office
Free of UK income tax and CGT	At least 14 working days. No interest if repaid in first year	*Buy:* application form available through post offices, to be sent to Savings Certificate Office *Sell:* on written application to Savings Certificate Office

WHERE TO FIND OUT MORE

Banks and money funds
Local branches for banks: the newspapers for money funds.

Building societies
The Building Societies Association (01-437 0655) can answer questions of a general nature. They also public a range of booklets and leaflets about societies, but cannot advise on which societies are offering the best rates.

Building Society Choice is available on subscription only from *MoneyGuide,* Rattlesden, Bury St Edmonds, Suffolk IP30 OSF. Published monthly, it provides a summary of the best rates available.

National Savings
Information available at post offices.
General telephone enquiries to 01-605 9461 (Mondays to Fridays, 9am to 4pm).
For information on the latest interest rates for Income Bonds, Deposit Bonds and Investment Accounts, there is a 24-hour Ansafone service:
South: 01-605 9483 or 01-605 9484
North: 0253-723714;
Scotland: 041-632 2766.

CHAPTER 3

FIXED CAPITAL INVESTMENTS (II)

Chapter 2 dealt with the main organisations offering fixed capital investment, but there are some further choices. The first of these are local authorities who, like the Government, need to raise money from time to time to supplement their revenue from the rates.

Local authorities issue two types of security. The first are 'Negotiable Bonds' which can last from one to five years. The majority last for a year and hence are known as 'yearlings'. These bonds can be traded on the Stock Exchange. They behave like gilts rather than fixed capital bonds as their capital value can fluctuate and, as such, belong more to the next chapter than to this one. The second type of local authority issues are 'Local Authority Mortgage Bonds' often simply called local authority loans. They are issued for fixed periods of one to ten years and are non-negotiable (i.e, they cannot be bought by or sold to third parties) and the capital value does not fluctuate.

Local authority bonds are assumed to be more or less as safe as any Government-backed investment, simply because it is assumed that the Government would back up any local authority which was in danger of defaulting. In fact, there is no legal commitment for the Government to do so (and there have been examples to prove this, notably, in recent times, Liverpool), but the loss of political face that would be involved in refusing to help makes it extremely unlikely that investors would ever suffer a total loss.

The minimum investment in local authority loans ranges from £250 to £10,000 or so, depending on the authority concerned and the term. There are over 200 local authorities (from Adur District Council to Yeovil) and at any one time at least half of them may be looking for money.

The place to get information on what is on offer is the CIPFA Loans Bureau based at Colechurch House, 1 London Bridge Walk, London SE1. The Bureau collates details of all the bonds available on a weekly basis. Professional advisers such as solicitors can subscribe to receive the list every week, or single copies can be purchased for £2.50.

Alternatively, the Loans Bureau runs a telephone enquiry

service (01-407 2767). If you know the amount you want to invest and the number of years you are willing to tie it up for, the Bureau will tell you what the highest offerings are that week.

Table 13 Local authority loans

Typical rates (net of composite tax)	Years						
	1 %	2 %	3 %	4/5 %	6/7 %	9 %	10 %
	6.7	7.25	7.25	7.25	7.25	7.25	7.25

Table 13 shows some typical rates as we go to press. The interest rates are fixed, not variable, and are now paid net of composite rate tax (though holders of bonds issued before 19 November 1984 still receive interest gross).

The rates offered on the bonds are usually competitive with what can be obtained elsewhere, but you do have to remember that it is not usually possible to get your money back before the end of the quoted term, whatever emergency or disaster may befall, while by virtue of the fact that the interest rate is fixed, you may lose out if rates subsequently rise.

GUARANTEED INCOME AND GROWTH BONDS

These bonds are issued by life assurance companies. They generally require a minimum investment of £1,000 or more but last for a fixed term (two to ten years: four and five years are the most common) and offer a fixed rate of interest which is paid net of basic rate tax.

Guaranteed Bonds are a 'now you see it now you don't' sort of investment. Generally, limited offers are made, for limited periods of time. If you do not get in while the offer is open, you may have to wait some time before another offer is made. The reason for this relates to the tax position of the life company concerned: the mechanics are complicated, but the end result is that life companies can only offer a finite amount during each tax year without jeopardising their tax position. It is then a marketing decision on their part as to whether to spread them throughout the tax year, or use up the whole amount in one swoop.

The rates they can offer are based on the returns available from gilts and – depending on the market – they will sometimes pre-buy the gilts, so as to be able to offer higher rates than are available elsewhere in the market two or three weeks hence. Table 14 gives some examples at time of writing.

Table 14 Examples of Guaranteed Income Bond rates

Term	Income net of basic rate tax %
1 year	6.7 to 7.0
2 years	6.6
3 years	7.9
4 years	7.5
5 years	6.75 to 8.5

Note: For comparison, these bonds were available when the pattern of interest rates on competing products were as follows:

Product	Term or notice required	Rate net of basic rate tax %	Interest fixed or variable
NS Certificates 33rd issue	5 years	7.0*	fixed
NS Income Bond	3 months	7.67	variable
Building Society Instant access (minimum £5,000)	none	7.5 to 7.75	variable
Building Society 90 day account (minimum £10,000)	3 months	up to 8.25	variable

* Tax free to all investors

If you are prepared to tie up your capital for a fixed period of years, guaranteed bonds are often a good deal, as they frequently manage to offer higher rates than building societies (indeed, they usually time their offers to make sure they do).

The income bonds usually pay income once yearly though sometimes they offer a monthly income facility if you invest say £10,000 or more. One point to watch out for is what happens to the income payment should the bondholder die. This type of bond is often taken out by elderly people, so the point is relevant. Some will not pay out any proportionate income at all, even if the bondholder dies a few days before the next payment is due. Another area to watch, despite the fact that the bonds are often bought by married couples, is that some are set up only on a 'single life' basis, so if the husband dies, his widow who might have been expecting the income payment as usual, finds she receives nothing – just the capital returned. If it is allowed, the only sensible way is to take out a bond like this on a 'joint life, last survivor' basis – and preferably, choose one that would pay out the full, porportionate income. But this option may mean a slightly lower level of income, so you will have to weigh up the alternatives.

'Growth' bonds are simply a variation on the same theme: instead of paying the interest out each year, it is rolled-up in the bond so that you receive back an enhanced capital sum at the end of the period. The profit counts as income and is taxed as such rather than capital gain.

TAX POSITION

The mechanics of income and growth bonds are fiendishly complicated. But basically they are in three categories:
1 A non-qualifying single premium endowment policy with guaranteed bonuses;
2 A non-qualifying annual premium endowment policy with guaranteed bonuses;
3 A combination of a temporary annuity plus a deferred annuity.

How these actually work need be of no concern to the investor, with one importat caveat. If you are a basic rate taxpayer, the mechanics used will make no difference to the net return you receive.

But if you are a higher rate taxpayer, or someone whose income is around the level where you might be caught by the 'age allowance trap' (see Chapter 13) then the actual mechanics of the bond can affect the amount of extra tax you will pay. A good insurance broker or other professional adviser should be able to help here.

Guaranteed bond offers are usually advertised in the papers and/or mentioned in articles. Most are offered by UK life companies and thus come under the protection of the Policyholders Protection Act (90 per cent of your money back if the life company fails). Some bonds are issued by 'offshore' life companies based in places such as the Isle of Man, the Channel Islands or Gibraltar. While one does not want to tar them all with the same brush, it is true that there have been some spectacular failures of offshore life companies, which have resulted in investors losing all their money. If you are considering investing in an offshore guaranteed bond, do it through a registered broker and ask his advice first.

CERTIFICATES OF TAX DEPOSIT

This scheme is operated by the Inland Revenue. If you have large tax bills to face in the future, you may deposit the money with them in advance where it will earn interest in the meantime. The rate of interest depends on the time you invest and also on whether you actually use the money for paying tax.

As I write, the interest rate for deposits of £100,000 or less is 8.0 per cent if the money is used in settlement of a scheduled tax liability, but only 5 per cent if it is withdrawn for cash. The interest rate on these deposits can change quite frequently, but one you have made your deposit, the rate applying on the date of the deposit applies to your investment for the whole of the next year. It is then revised to whatever rate is in force on each anniversary thereafter.

Interest on these certificates will continue to be paid gross – but, of course, they are of no use to the non-taxpayer because the interest rate is so much less if they are not used for paying tax! Information on the scheme and current interest rates are available from any Inland Revenue Collecting Office.

OFFSHORE MONEY FUNDS

These are the offshore equivalent of the money market funds described in Chapter 2, with some important differences. The currency concerned need not be sterling: it is possible to invest in funds that are denominated in US dollars, deutschmarks, Swiss francs, French francs, Dutch guilders or Japanese yen. A rather different animal is the 'Managed Currency Fund' where the managers will swop about between different currencies, hoping to make gains on the exchange rates. In either case, the 'foreign money' funds involve a risk to your capital, as where currency gains are to be had, naturally, losses can also arise.

Sterling offshore funds
The sterling offshore funds are more closely related to the on-

shore money funds as they both tend to invest in the same things: low risk instruments such as bank deposits, Certificates of Deposits and other money market instruments.

TAX TREATMENT

The tax treatment, however, is completely different. There are two types of money offshore fund for tax purposes: they can have 'distributor' or 'accumulator' status. To understand the distinction it is worth looking at the past history of these funds.

Until the end of 1983, offshore money funds (dubbed 'roll-up' funds) enjoyed a marvellous time at the expense of the Inland Revenue. The interest earned on the money invested was not distributed to investors, but was 'rolled up' within the fund, and when the investor sold his holding, he was assessed for Capital Gains Tax (CGT), rather than income tax, on his profits. With CGT at a maximum of 30 per cent and the annual £6,000 plus exemption from the tax available to all individuals, 'roll-up' funds were obviously an excellent place for your money – particularly for higher rate taxpayers.

It was too good to last, and the Revenue stepped in with a new set of rules. From January 1984, offshore funds were faced with a choice: they could either apply for 'distributor' status, which meant they had to distribute at least 85 per cent of their income, and on which their investors would be taxed at income tax rates; or they could continue to be 'accumulator' (i.e. 'roll-up') funds, but in this case, all the profits, when cashed by the investor, would be assessed at income tax rates. This would be pretty hard for the foreign currency and managed funds, as some of their profits arise from genuine capital gains rather than interest.

Sterling roll-up funds still have their good points though. The basic point in their favour is that they allow you to defer tax, even though you do not avoid it completely. This can be especially useful if you know that your tax rate will fall at some point in the future, after retirement, for example. But even for people whose tax rate remains the same, the roll-up alternative has the advantage that you can continue to earn interest on the money that will one day have to be handed over to the taxman, which, for higher rate taxpayers in particular, can be quite advantageous.

It has been calculated that if a fund is earning 10 per cent gross, the effective rate of tax for a 60 per cent taxpayer holding an investment for 5 years would be reduced to 49 per cent, and 33 per cent if he kept his holding intact for 15 years.

This system is fine if you do not actually want the interest to spend. If you do, the system can still work in your favour. Instead of withdrawing all the interest (as you would do, for example, with a building society account or with a distributor fund) while leaving the capital intact, you simply cash in a number of shares in the fund, equivalent to the net interest your entire holding has earned. You will pay some tax, certainly, but most of the proceeds you are actually getting consist of your capital on which no tax is payable.

People who are in the 'age allowance' trap could find this method leaves them with a higher spendable income than, for example, if they kept their savings in a building society, and though it is marginally less convenient, it is effectively as risk-free.

The minimum investment in these funds varies between £1,000 and £10,000. There is one drawback to the funds, which is that they all charge an annual management fee. For the best returns it is advisable to go for one that has an annual charge of 0.75 per cent or less.

WHERE TO FIND OUT MORE

Guaranteed income and growth bonds
See the financial pages of newspapers (editorial and advertising) for details of current offers, or consult an insurance broker or other professional adviser.

Certificates of tax deposit
Information available at any Inland Revenue collecting office.

Sterling roll-up funds
See the financial pages of newspapers and specialist magazines or consult a financial adviser.

STRENGTH IN NUMBERS

PROFESSIONAL SERIES	POSITION IN SECTOR	% INCREASE
Japan Growth	1st	+250.0
Far East Growth	1st	+204.4
American Growth	3rd	+ 46.8
European Growth	3rd	+132.0
American Income	8th	+ 37.2
International Growth	14th	+ 95.6
UK Income	24th	+111.7
UK Growth	50th	+108.0
MANAGED SERIES		
Managed High Yield	1st	+221.9
Managed Growth	1st	+176.0
Managed Income	1st	+146.1

(All statistics MicrOpal offer to bid for the 25 months since launch to 1.7.87)

As you can see above, the performance of our unit trusts is quite impressive. An investment of £1,000 made at launch in the Sun Life Japan Growth Portfolio will have increased in value to £3,500.

To find out what's behind this success contact your professional advisor or complete the coupon below.

To: Sun Life Trust Management Limited, Granite House, 101 Cannon Street, London EC4N 5AD.
☐ Please send me more information on the full range of Sun Life unit trusts.
☐ I would like a representative to call me.

Name_____

Address_____

_____ Phone _____

SN DTLSI 9/87

SUN LIFE UNIT TRUSTS

CHAPTER 4

THE GILTS MARKET

THE BACKGROUND

Mr Micawber's philosophy – that if annual income was £20 and annual expenditure £20 6d, the result was misery – has never appealed much to the Government of this country, or anywhere else for that matter. For the last 300 years governments have not been able to make ends meet and they have not shown much inclination to try either – they borrow instead. In 1914 the National Debt, as these borrowings are called, stood at £650 million. Today, the total stands at over £120 billion. So do not leave any of your money to reduce it, it simply is not worth it and the Government is scarcely a worthy beneficiary of such thrifty thought!

The vast bulk of the borrowings made by the Government consist of gilt-edged securities. National savings products are another means by which the Government borrows money off us, but they form a relatively small proportion of the total. 'Gilts' – so-called because in the old days the certificates were edged in gold – come in all shapes and sizes, the oldest in issue dating back to 1752.

The essential feature of gilts is that they are negotiable securities: they can, in other words, be bought and sold by third parties. There are about 100 different stocks in issue and the amount of trading that goes on in the gilts market is phenomenal. In 1984, for example, the average *daily* trading in gilts ran at around £1,000 million.

WHAT INFLUENCES GILTS PRICES?

The prices of gilts are affected by all sort of factors, including political and even psychological ones. Ultimately, however, they respond to movements in interest rates – and often, since the market tends to be one step ahead, to *expectations* of movements in interest rates. And since interest rates cannot be considered in isolation from the inflation rate they are influenced by that – and likewise, by inflationary expectations rather than the (backward looking) Retail Price Index.

When interest rates fall, the prices of gilts rise, and when rates rise, gilt prices fall. Figure 2 shows how it works in practice, though as you can see, the prices of gilts are more erratic and volatile than shifts in interest rates.

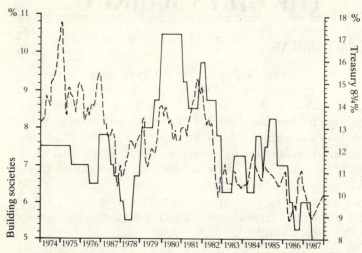

Figure 2 Treasury 8 3/4% 1997 – Red. Yield from 1/1/74 to 14/8/87 monthly
Source: *Datastream*
UK interest rate paid by Building Societies on ordinary shares percentage.
Source: Building Societies Association   Source: *Datastream*

Key
- - - Treasury 8 3/4%
—— Building society rate

THE TERMS

The gilts market abounds in technical terms. The name of any particular gilt is the least important thing about it. These days, most gilts are called 'Exchequer' or 'Treasury' but there are others with names such as British Gas or British Transport (issued to pay for the nationalisation of their respective industries) and War Loan. The other component parts of the description of any one stock will tell you some things, but not a lot. For example, 'Exchequer 10 1/2% 1988' tells you firstly that the stock will be redeemed (paid back) in 1988, and secondly that the interest rate (the 'coupon') per £100 of nominal stock is 10.5 per cent a year. 'Coupon' incidentally is another historical oddity, dating back to the days when certificates had a series of tear-off slips which you posted away to receive the interest.

Prices of gilts are always quoted 'per £100 nominal', the 'nominal' being what the Government will repay once redemption date arrives. This is also known as the 'par value' or 'face value'. In the meantime the price of the gilt will move according to the market. As I write this, for instance 'Exchequer 9¾% 1987' cost '£97½' (gilts prices are traditionally quoted in fractions) per £100 nominal, standing below par value in other words.

Obviously, if you are buying £100-worth for rather less than £100, you are getting more interest for your money than the 9.75 per cent of the coupon. The gross 'interest yield' (also known as the 'flat' or 'running' yield) is arrived at by taking the price of the gilt into account, and in this case works out at 9.99 per cent.

There is a further factor to take into account. Remember that when it is redeemed in 1997, holders receive back the full £100, so there is an in-built profit of £2.50 to be picked up at that point, which increases the overall yield. The gross redemption yield – as this is known – on this particular stock at time of writing is 10.11 per cent. Further examples of the different yields relating to different stocks are shown in Table 16, including some that are standing above par at time of writing.

The range of gilts available can be categorised in separate ways by the amount of time they have to run before redemption, and by the coupon. 'Gas 3% 1990-5' is an example of a 'low coupon' stock, 'Treasury 15¼% 1996' is a 'high coupon' stock.

As far as redemption dates are concerned, short-dated gilts or 'shorts' are those that have less than five years to run before maturity. The prices of these gilts are the least volatile of all stocks, because the nearer you get to redemption date, the closer the price of the gilt will move to its nominal or par value.

Medium-dated stocks have redemption dates between five and fifteen years away and 'longs' are redeemable in more than fifteen years' time. Medium-dated and long-dated stocks are more volatile in their price movements than shorts; they do not, so to speak, have the sobering influence of a rapidly approaching redemption date to dampen down the price movements. Some gilts show two redemption dates ('Gas 3% 1990-95'). This means that the Government can redeem the stock at any time between the two dates, normally the latest possible date is chosen.

Then there are the 'undated stocks' – a clutch of five different stocks which the Government has theoretically promised

Table 15 Gross redemption yields on gifts

Stock	Price	Yield %
Treasury 5% 1986–9	93⁷/₃₂	8.50
Treasury 13% 1990	106¹/₁₆	10.06
Gas 3% 1990-5	83	5.77
Treasury 15¹/₄% 1996	128¹/₁₆	10.27
Treasury 10¹/₂% 1999	102³/₄	10.05

to pay back, but has omitted to mention when. Going by 'Consols 2¹/₂%', the most realistic answer is 'never': this is the stock mentioned earlier, first issued in 1752, which has not *yet* been redeemed.

There is one rather different category of gilts: index-linked stocks, such as 'Treasury 2% 1988'. The rules are completely different here. Both the repayment of the capital and the payments of interest in the meantime are guaranteed to rise in line with inflation.

This does not mean their price cannot fluctuate like conventional gilts – it can and does. At the time of writing, several of the index-linked gilts stand below par, reflecting investors' views that the 2 per cent or 2.5 per cent 'real' interest rate these gilts offer (at par value) is not particularly attractive when you compare it to the 5 per cent or more 'real' interest yield obtainable on conventional gilts. As index-linked gilts get closer towards their redemption date, their price will not, of course, move towards £100, but towards whatever the index-linked value will be.

GILTS AND TAX

There are two basis rules affecting individual investors.
1 Interest received from a gilt is taxable as income. Interest is generally paid net of basic rate (27 per cent) tax, with the exception of War Loan and stocks that are bought through the Post Office (see 'How to buy and sell' on page 60). Non-taxpayers can reclaim the tax, though it is likely to be more convenient for them to go for the gilts that pay interest gross by effecting their purchases via the Post Office.
2 Profits made from rises in the price of gilts are taxed as capital gains with a very important exception: profits made

from gilts held for more than a year are exempt from the tax.

The consequence of these rules can be clearly seen in Table 17, which illustrates the *net* redemption yields of various gilts at different rates of tax. The higher the rate of tax you pay, the more beneficial it is for you to go for a 'low coupon' gilt, where the bulk of your profits will come not from the (taxable) interest you receive but from the (tax-free) final gain you make on redemption.

Table 16 Net redemption yields on gilts

Stock	Price	Gross redemption yield %	Net redemption yields at following tax rates:			
			27%	40%	50%	60%
British Transport 3% 1979–88	96.75	6.89	6.06	5.66	5.36	5.05
Funding 6% 1993	87.43	8.70	6.95	6.11	5.46	4.81
Exchequer 11% 1990	101.78	10.15	7.22	5.81	4.72	3.64
Treasury 9% 1994	95.47	9.88	7.38	6.18	5.25	4.33
Exchequer 12% 1998	112.0	10.17	7.18	5.73	4.62	3.50
Treasury 13¼% 1997	118.15	10.195	7.00	5.46	4.26	3.07

Source: *Capel Cure Myers*

The net redemption yield is the most important measure for an individual to use in deciding which stock to buy. Most stockbrokers now have computer systems to enable them to reel off the net redemption yields at any given tax rate for any gilt.

PAYMENT OF INTEREST

Interest payments on gilts are all made (with a single exception) twice a year. There are special arrangements to reflect the fact that when a gilt is sold, it will have a certain number of days' accrued interest within it. If you sell a stock shortly before the interest payment is due, for instance, it is worth more to the buyer at that point than it would be if he had bought it immediately after you had taken that interest payment.

But there is another time factor involved. The Bank of England needs a certain number of days to prepare and send off the interest payments. If stocks are being bought and sold right up to the last minute, the Bank would have no idea who the interest payment belongs to. So a system has arisen whereby 37 days before an interest payment is due, the stock goes 'ex dividend' (noted with the sign 'xd' after it). This means any buyer after that time foregoes the right to the next interest payment (which is sent to the seller).

There is one further ramification here. For stocks with 5 years or more to run, there is a further period of 21 days before the 37 days start where buyers and sellers have a choice: they can sell (buy) the stock *special ex dividend or cum dividend*.

For income tax purposes, however, all this is irrelevant. Interest is treated as accruing on a day-to-day basis, which means that whenever a gilt is sold, the seller must pay income tax on the exact days' worth of interest he was entitled to by virtue of owning that stock. The only exception to the above rules is for investors who hold less than £5,000 nominal stock (in total).

In this situation, holders are only liable to income tax on the income that they have actually received; if they sold the gilt shortly before it was due to go 'xd', any profits made are treated as capital gains, not income, for tax purposes. It's a nice loophole, but not a large one, and given the bother and expense of dealing, it's frankly not really worth doing for most people. Basic rate taxpayers would almost certainly be better off simply leaving that money in a high interest building society account.

GILTS AND THE PRIVATE INVESTOR

The vast bulk of trading that is done in gilts is carried out by the institutions: life assurance companies, pensions funds and the like. However, it is perfectly possible for individuals to buy gilts directly, either via a stockbroker or the Post Office. The most popular category of gilts with the private investor are medium-dated stocks. 'Longs', with redemption dates at least 15 years away, are simply too long for most individuals to be bothered with.

Investors can, if they wish, buy a gilt and hold it to maturity. This way, they get absolute certainty. Their motives for doing so can be either to provide themselves with a guaranteed income, and/or a guaranteed gain.

Income seekers who are not worried about effectively spending some of their capital to get it can go for high coupon stocks where the price is currently standing above par. 'Treasury 14½% 1994' is one such example at time of writing:

its price is '120$^{3/16}$ xd', meaning that there is a guaranteed capital *loss* building up for its holder as in 1994 he will only get back £100 for every £120.19 he spends now. In exchange for this, he is getting a gross interest yield of 12.05 per cent a year.

This tactic is worse than useless for the higher rate taxpayer who would be heavily taxed on the income received. He is more likely to go for a low coupon stock which has a guaranteed capital *gain* on maturity, which will (assuming he has held it for more than a year) be tax-free, while the low level of income he receives in the meantime will not worry him, as it will only be taxed to ribbons anyway.

A middle of the road, basic rate taxpayer might go for a combination: something like 'Treasury 9% 1994', which will cost him, in August 1987, '95$^{9/32}$', giving him a gross interest yield of 9.46 per cent plus a guaranteed capital gain (albeit small) on maturity.

But would any of these individuals be wise to do so? Choosing an investment always means choosing between the relative merits of competing products. A long term building society account could, for example, give the basic rate taxpayer a much higher immediate net return, even if there is no corresponding capital gain to be made.

This bring us to the most important point to be made about gilts: it is essential to time your investments properly. If you look back at Figure 2 on page 42, you will see that gilt prices tend to rise as (or just before) interest rates fall. What investors should be aiming to do is to move from fixed capital deposit type investments (bank deposits, building society accounts) once interest rates look as if they are in a downtrend, and make the move back again as interest rates rise.

In this, the gilts market differs somewhat from the equity market. With shares, though timing certainly plays a part; it is, if anything, even more important that you pick the right shares: it is possible (though harder) to make gains in a falling equity market, so long as you have picked the right shares. With gilts, on the other hand, although 'stock selection' plays a part, assuming you have followed the pretty basic ground rules outlined above (low coupon gilts for higher rate taxpayers, medium-sized or high coupon gilts for basic rate and non-taxpayers), the particular stock you have selected will not perform that much differently from its fellow stocks. Timing, by contrast, can make the crucial difference.

CONVENTIONAL GILTS VERSUS INDEX-LINKED GILTS

So far, this chapter has concentrated mainly on conventional gilts (those that pay a fixed rate of interest and guarantee to pay back the nominal amount on maturity) as opposed to index-linked gilts. There is a choice; but on what basis should you choose?

You will simply have to use your judgement as to what you think is happening to inflation. In a sense, index-linked gilts (and their National Savings equivalent, index-linked certicates) are the most certain of all forms of investment as they guarantee a *real* return on your capital which is itself guaranteed to retain exactly the purchasing power it possessed when you invested. By contrast, the guarantee on nominal returns, such as is offered by conventional gilts held to maturity, as well as by the fixed capital investments described in Chapters 2 and 3, is a guarantee without teeth, a very partial guarantee at best.

But this is not to say that index-linked investments are the automatic answer for any investor, even the least audacious or (which often accompanies this) the poorest investor. Ironically, index-linked gilts favour the higher rate taxpayer because they are, in this respect, like low coupon gilts, as the bulk of the 'profit' comes from growth in the capital value, not interest.

One of the tools that stockbrokers have devised for judging the relative attractions of index-linked versus conventional gilts is the 'break-even inflation rate'. What you do (or, rather, what a stockbroker with a computer does) is pick the best conventional gilt for your tax rate, and 'match' it to an index-linked gilt maturing in the same year. You then work out what the inflation rate would have to average over the intervening period for the index-linked gilt to provide a return which in monetary terms equals the return from the conventional gilt.

So, for example, as we went to print, 'Treasury 9% 1992–96' offered a net redemption yield of 6.14 per cent for a basic (27 per cent) rate taxpayer. If 'Treasury 2% 1996' (the nearest index-linked gilt) was to produce a similar return, inflation would have to run at 3.209 per cent a year between now and then – any higher, and you would be ahead with the index-linked gilt.

The 'break-even inflation rate' trick does not remove the

need for your own judgement but it does help to concentrate the mind. Many stockbrokers are now making use of the concept, and if you are a higher rate taxpayer in particular, it could well be worthwhile finding out the relvant figures at the time you are thinking of investing.

HOW TO BUY AND SELL GILTS

Gilts can be bought in two ways: direct through post offices or via a stockbroker. The advantage to buying through the Post Office is:
(a) It is relatively cheap (see Table 17);
(b) Interest is received gross.

The disadvantages are:
(c) Only a certain number of issues are on the 'National Savings Stock Register' and can be bought in this way – a leaflet is available from the Post Office which gives a list of which ones are available;
(d) Both purchases and sales take longer than carrying out the transaction through a stockbroker and you do not know (until after the event) what price you have bought at.

Table 17 The cost of buying gilts through the Post Office

Purchases, cost of transaction	Commission charged
Not exceeding £250	£1
Over £250	£1 and a further 50p for every additional £125 (or part)
Sales; amount realised	Commission charged
Less than £100	10p for every £10 (or part)
£100–£250	£1
Over £250	£1 and a further 50p for every additional £125 (or part)

If you want to receive interest gross, what you can do is apply to transfer your holding on to the National Savings Stock Register after you have bought it. However, you are only allowed to transfer £5,000 nominal of any particular stock in this way in any calendar year.

If you are buying through a stockbroker, the cost depends totally on how much you are investing. In theory, gilts are cheaper to buy than equities, and for large sums this is indeed the case; most firms now charge private clients commission of 1.65% for equities but only 0.8% for gilts.

But smaller purchases run up against the minimum commission that all brokers charge: a minimum that, for a London-based firm, is unlikely to be less than £15 (and often more) and, if you're lucky, perhaps £12 in the provinces. VAT is payable on the broker's commission, though unlike equities, purchases of gilts do not attract stamp duty.

When you bear in mind you must pay commission both when you buy and when you sell, you should ideally be thinking in terms of at least £1,000 or £2,000 per stock to make the exercise worthwhile.

An alternative for smaller investors who want to invest in gilts (but not for those insisting on the certainty of holding stocks to maturity) is a gilt unit trust or single premium life assurance bond where you can buy into a portfolio of gilts much more cheaply than would be possible by going direct.

WHERE TO FIND OUT MORE

Papers such as the *Daily Telegraph* and *Financial Times* publish lists of all Government securities every day, giving both the gross interest yield and gross redemption yield.

For calculations of net redemption yields at particular rates of tax, as well as for advice on which stocks to buy or sell, a stockbroker is the best bet.

CHAPTER 5

EQUITIES

This now brings us to UK equities and the London Stock Exchange, although much of what is going to be said applies equally to investments in shares listed on other exchanges. For the majority of investors, however, the costs and practical difficulties of buying foreign shares directly are such that it is likely to be both easier and cheaper to do so by means of a pooled investment vehicle such as a unit or investment trust.

THE STOCK EXCHANGE

The first concept of shares in a company, and the notion of 'limited liability' that goes along with it, date back to Elizabethan times. The typical example always quoted concerns ships trading overseas: a number of merchants would get together to finance a particular voyage and then share in the profits when their ship eventually returned. From this it was a short step to being able to sell your share to some interested buyer if you did not want to wait until the ship returned to port. It gradually became apparent that it was not necessary to set up a separate arrangement for each voyage which was unwound once the trip was completed, you could have a permanent 'company' instead.

The obvious place for the meetings to be held to arrange the financing deals, and to exchange shares, was close to the river. The market grew up in the coffee houses round the Royal Exchange – hence the term 'waiter', still used for the Stock Exchange attendants. In 1773, one particular coffee house, New Jonathan's, became the recognised place to meet and was the first building in the world to be called 'The Stock Exchange'. It was formally constituted in 1802; a year earlier, a purpose-built home for it had been constructed; its successor, the new Stock Exchange building, was opened in 1973 on the same site.

Today, less than a year after the Stock Exchange's 'Big Bang', the floor of the Stock Exchange is deserted. Everyone knows of the Big Bang, but probably few people can remember what it was actually all about.

Three major changes happened in the organisation of the stock exchange in 1986: first, the structure of minimum commissions charged for buying and selling shares was demolished; secondly, stockbroking and jobbing firms were allowed to be taken over by companies, rather than being partnerships as before; and thirdly, the two different functions of jobbing and broking were allowed to take place within one company, under one roof.

These two separate functions remain, however, and are fundamental to the way shares are bought and sold. The jobber, now called the market maker, is the wholesaler: he keeps a stock of shares on his books, and deals only with the broker, not with end customers. The broker takes orders from, and advises, his customers, and tours the market makers (these days, by checking up on a screen on his desk, rather than wandering round the stock exchange floor) to get the best price for his shares, whether he's buying or selling.

Where the two functions are carried out under one roof, there is supposed to be a 'Chinese Wall' between them, so the left hand does not know what the right is doing. Otherwise there would be the temptation to off-load onto some ignorant customer shares that the market maker want to get rid of.

Since the Big Bang, the volume of shares traded has shot up, and brokers everywhere have been drowning in a mass of paperwork. Investors large and small have had to put up with extremely lengthy delays in getting certificates of shares they have bought, or (worse) money for shares they have sold. The only people who are smiling are the back-room administrators who for years have seen their colleagues in the dealing rooms earn fantastic salaries, while they have been largely unappreciated. Now it's their turn for the limelight and the big salary increases.

The main effect for the small investor of the Big Bang has been an increase in dealing costs. Not a large one, but there has been a noticeable creep upwards in the minimum commission charged. Some London-based brokers now charge a minimum £30 for handling a sale or purchase, however small; and while provincial brokers are likely to be slightly cheaper, £15 to £20 is the 'going rate' these days. What it means in effect is that unless you are buying or selling shares in parcels of say £1,000 each, the exercise can begin to be uneconomic.

Despite these changes in the way the Stock Exchange works, its functions have remained exactly the same. In fact there are two, quite distinct functions: to raise new capital for companies largely by issuing new share capital, and to act as a marketplace for people wanting to buy and sell existing shares. As regards the latter activity, the companies themselves receive no direct benefit from the transactions that then take place, though a healthy share price should mean that it will be easier for them to raise fresh capital as and when they need to.

Table 18 UK Stock Exchange: facts and figures

	£m	
Total equity market value	473,719	
Total pre-tax profits	21,666	
Total number of UK companies listed		2,173
Unlisted Securities Market		
Total equity market value	8,314	
Total pre-tax profits	285	
Total number of companies		367
Third Market		
Total equity market value	128	
Total number of companies		22

Source: *The Stock Exchange*
Note: All figures are as of June 1987, the latest available at the time of going to print.

The main Stock Exchange has been joined, in recent years, by a couple of smaller siblings – the Unlisted Securities Market (USM) and The 3rd Market. The distinguishing feature of the three markets is the nature of the rules and regulations companies must follow before their shares are eligible to be traded on that market. The USM has less onerous rules than the main market, and the third market less than the second. The third market, for example, can accommodate companies which have not yet begun trading.

It should be obvious that shares quoted on the USM or third market are likely to be a more risky proposition than fully-listed shares; but it is worth bearing in mind that the increased risk is not simply due to the fact that the companies involved are younger, smaller and with less of a track record.

While you may be willing to take this investment risk, there is also the factor of *market liquidity:* whether you can buy (or perhaps more importantly, sell) the shares when you want to. Remember that the major players in the stock market these days are, like it or not, the big institutions, and they may simply not be interested in a company in which, however bright its prospects, they cannot invest more than a very small amount.

Hovering in the background is the 'grey market': not a market at all in a formal sense. Some dealers are willing to make a market in shares that have no formal connection with the stock exchange.

One group of characters you would do well to ignore are the share pushing companies, invariably based offshore, who by newsletter or telephone calls try to persuade investors to put money into little known (or probably completely unknown) shares which they just happen to be making a market in. There are crooks galore in this game: avoid them like the plague.

Table 18 shows a few more facts and figures about the Stock Exchange and the USM.

THE PRIVATE INVESTOR

The role of the private investor in the Stock Exchange has in fact been one of continuous decline since the heady days of the early 1960s, when well over half the shares in issue were held by individuals, as Table 19 shows. Two factors in particular are pointed to as reasons for this. Firstly, the tax situation was for many years positively hostile towards the private shareholder; secondly, the (not unconnected) massive rise in the purchasing power of the institutions, pensions funds in particular.

But while the institutions will continue to dominate the Stock Exchange thanks to their massive purchasing power, there has been an abrupt about-turn in the number of individuals who are willing to have a go and become shareholders. Thanks to the tax-free, practically risk-free bonanza of the privatisations (British Telecom, Gas, British Airways and so on) the number of individuals who have become shareholders has rocketed in the last couple of years or so. It is now estimated that 8.5 million people now hold shares directly – around 19.6 of the adult population.

I have mixed feelings about the policy of privatisations. It was meant to turn us all into shareholders, so we would have a direct stake in the economic well-being of the country, in the same way as, by turning into a nation of property owners, we have a stake in our environment.

I've nothing against the theory; in practice, though, I wonder whether it has turned us into a nation of punters rather than shareholders, who see an excursion into the Stock Exchange as a pleasing (and probably more remunerative) alternative to the pools or horse-racing. That is all very well, but it completely misses the point of what investment is supposed to be about. And the problem is that, after their first successful foray into shares, people seem to think this sort of exercise can be easily repeated and go straight from a privatisation into buying shares of unlisted companies on the advice of some newsletter dropped through their door, and see no difference in the degree of risk they are undertaking.

Perhaps the moral to be drawn from this is that there is, sometimes, such a thing as a free lunch in investment terms – and the government has undoubtedly provided us with a succession of picnic baskets at no charge. But then it's had one (or several – and not necessarily bad) ulterior motives for doing so. It is as well to remember, in the general run of things, that people usually want to make money for themselves, first.

A little bit of cynicism is a fair way to start, but even better would be a larger amount of knowledge. So let's begin with the basics.

Table 19 Decline of the private shareholder?

	1963 %	1975 %	1979 %	1981 %	1986 %
Institutional holdings (pension funds, insurance companies, units and investments trusts, etc.)	27.8	46.9	51.5	57.9	65.0
Persons	58.7	37.5	32.5	28.2	18.0
Charities, Government, overseas, and others	13.5	15.6	16.0	13.9	17.0
Value £ bn	£27.5	£44.6	£70.0	£92.0	£231.0

Source: *Phillips & Drew*.
1981 figures issued by Stock Exchange.
1986 figures Phillips & Drew estimate.

WHAT IS AN ORDINARY SHARE?

Companies are distinct legal entities in their own right but they always have owners – their shareholders. A share is quite literally a share in the ownership of the company.

All companies that are listed on the Stock Exchange are 'limited liability' companies. This means that should the company incur massive debts it cannot meet, the shareholders are only liable to the extent that the share is 'partly paid' – in other words, if the shareholders have not contributed the full amount on each share then they have to pay the difference in their 'partly paid' shares at this time. This is not relevant in the vast majority of companies whose shares are bought and sold on the Stock Exchange, as they are 'fully paid' though it can occur in private companies. This is the extent of the limitation; shareholders can never lose more than they put in to the company, but they are at risk to that extent.

Ordinary shareholders stand last in line for getting anything back from the company if it goes into liquidation (first in line, in case you wondered, is the Inland Revenue – ordinary trade creditors are a good bit further back). The reward for taking the risk is that ordinary shareholders are entitled to the profits the company makes in the form of dividends. Most companies do not distribute all their profits to their shareholders, but retain some to plough back into the company itself, to retain its trading position or to grow.

Ordinary shareholders, too, are generally the only ones who have the right to vote at the company's general meetings: a fairly theoretical advantage, today's shareholders might feel, because unless they happen to have the investing power of a pension fund, they are unlikely to have enough shares to wield a significant vote.

WHY DO SHARES PRICES MOVE?

There are two positions from which one can attempt to answer this question: the bird's eye view and the worm's eye view. Investors will be aware of all the things that have a bearing on the general movement of the share price indices: general economic trends, political developments, strikes and trade figures. Even the good weather has been instanced as a reason for an upward trend! The market reports that many newspapers carry often seem to be talking about a person rather than the abstract entity of a market. 'Obstinately, the equity market refuses to emerge from its summer slumber' was the opening sentence of the *Financial Times'* weekly report on the UK market the day this chapter was being written.

But apart from generalised swings in the market, what makes particular share prices move? The trick answer to this is: 'the relative weight of supply and demand for the shares'. The stock market is often instanced as the (almost) perfect economic market, where supply and demand are the sole determinants of prices. The answer is a trick one because it does not give us any real information, it simply leads on immediately to the next question. What influences the level of supply and demand?

It boils down ultimately to a matter of profits; the rewards that an investor can expect to receive in the shape of rising dividends from a healthy company. From this it follows that there is also an expectation of capital growth: the value of the share will (it is hoped) rise as dividends continue on an upward trend. This is a second motive for investing; but although some individuals might be primarily interested in capital growth – this may be their main *personal* motive, as it were – it should not be forgotten that the shares themselves are ultimately judged solely on the prospects for their capacity to provide income. There are various criteria in use to judge the price of a particular share bearing in mind the level of dividends, which are detailed on the following pages.

DIVIDENDS AND HOW TO JUDGE THEM

UK companies usually declare their dividends in terms of 'pence per share' and the figure quoted is net of basic rate tax (non-taxpayers may reclaim this: higher rate taxpayers face an additional charge).

Dividends are usually paid twice a year: the 'interim' dividend and the 'final' dividend, paid after the end of the company's financial year. The company's announcements on either its interim or final dividend can obviously have an immediate effect on the share price. What often happens is that brokers engage in guessing games prior to the announcement and the share price moves in anticipation. So you can get a situation where a company announces an increased dividend and the share price falls because the increase is not as big as the market expected.

To digress slightly here, one of the rules of the Stock Exchange, which all listed companies have to obey, is that any 'price sensitive' information must be published immediately. Otherwise, a situation could arise where one person was taking an unfair advantage becase he knew something the others did not. 'Insider dealing' as this is called is forbidden and is now in fact a criminal offence.

DIVIDEND YIELD

This is the gross dividend expressed as a percentage of the share price: if the share is 100p, in other words, and the dividend is 6p, then the yield is 6 per cent. The yield on the FT-All Share Index is 3.06 per cent at time of writing. This is a lot lower than the yield you can currently obtain on gilts or other fixed interest investments: and has been, in fact, for the last 25 years. It used to be the other way round: gilts used to yield less than equities (hence the term 'the Yield Gap') but investors were content with this discrepancy because the gilts were totally safe. Then along came inflation. Investors realised that a yield which was capable of *growing* over the years was worth paying more for than one that did not. So what we have now is the 'Reverse Yield Gap', and to confuse the issue, it is sometimes shortened to 'Yield Gap'.

Different sectors of the economy tend to have different average levels of yield; companies in the mechanical engineering field, for instance, would tend to have higher yields than companies in the electrical sector because there are less prospects of growth in the long term for the mechanical engineering companies. Shares with a very high yield might have to be treated with caution: there could be a good reason why the market has valued them so low! In other words, you cannot judge a share simply by its yield in isolation from all other aspects.

DIVIDEND COVER

As noted earlier, companies do not necessarily pay out all the profits they earn but keep some back for reinvestment in the business. The more that the dividends are 'covered' by the total profit, the more safe that dividend is likely to be and the more scope there is for an increase in future years.

Sometimes companies will pay out more than they have actually made in one particular year, calling on retained profits from previous years to do so. This need not necessarily be a signal of disaster: many sectors have ups and downs over the years but companies deliberately try to smooth their dividend payments – but on the whole you are safer with one that is fully covered.

PRICE/EARNINGS RATIO

Another commonly used formula in assessing shares is the price/earnings ratio, often called the p/e for short. It is what it says, the price of the share divided by its earnings per share. The figure you get shows the number of years it would take the company, on its current earnings, to 'earn' its current share price. If people are extremely enthusiastic about the prospects for some particular company, and reckon that it is going to grow extremely fast, then they will bid up the price of the share so the p/e ratio could be 30 or 40. This has happened in the last year or two, particularly with small high technology orientated companies and this can be a warning signal. Conversely, a very low p/e ratio can also sound warning bells as this implies the share is deeply unloved by the market, so the share price is very low.

All these criteria come in two guises: historic and prospective. The former refers to the actual position of the company at its last balance sheet date, and the latter anticipates what the expected positions will be at the next one.

In general, the p/e ratio is one of the best tools for judging the relative cheapness (or otherwise) of shares. But you have to wield it fairly carefully. In the first place the average p/e varies widely for different sectors – the Financial Times publishes them daily (towards the back of the paper, under the heading 'FT-Actuaries Indices') and at time of writing, the sector of 'Agencies' had the highest rating, of 30.89, and Banks the lowest, of 7.59. So you should never consider the figure for one company in isolation from its sector.

Secondly, you should judge p/e ratios in the context of the general economy as well as thinking about the prospects for that particular company. For instance, ratios will tend to be lower when inflation is high: an obvious and logical point when you consider that the ratio is comparing the (real) money you pay out now for the shares, to the (inflated away) money you receive back in dividends over the coming years. The higher inflation is and is expected to remain, the lower the p/e ratio ought to be.

That is a very broad brush description of p/e ratios and how they work. Investment is not a science – or, to be more accurate, it is not a completely mechanistic process – because there are simply too many unknowns which one has to guess, or make a judgement about. But using tools like the p/e ratio can help you to get a broad 'feel' of whether the market is cheap or dear at any one time, and also to appreciate how particular companies are valued by the market.

HOW TO BUY AND SELL SHARES
BANK OR BROKER?

Few people have a family stockbroker these days, any more than they have a family solicitor. If you have never bought shares before, there are two routes you can choose: either via your bank or dealing directly with a broker.

Dealing through your bank is likely to be quicker in the first instance but could be more expensive: most banks are adopting the practice of charging their clients an extra £5 for share dealings (in addition to the commission that they split with the brokers) where the amount concerned is relatively small.

If you deal through a broker, though, you will have to wait until they have checked out your bank's reference. But unless you are only contemplating a one-off purchase – and as long as you are prepared for the delay the first time that you deal – it is probably much better to go for the broker straight away.

Unless you know or are recommended a particular firm, you should write to the Stock Exchange, London EC2 (or telephone 01-588 2355) and they will send you a list of brokers who are willing to take on new private client business. If you live anywhere in the provinces, you will be sent the complete list of all regional stockbrokers. If you live in London, you get a list of three. The reason they do not send out the entire list is, they say, that everyone would start at the top, which is fine for the As and Bs, rotten for the Ws to Zs. The Exchange rotates the list periodically and you are likely to get three firms all beginning with the same letter.

Many stockbrokers are now actively promoting their services, so watch out for their advertisements in specialist magazines and the personal finance pages of newspapers.

WHAT CAN A BROKER DO FOR YOU – AND WHAT DOES IT COST?

The quality of service and advice you can get is going to depend on who you go to and what you want. Several brokers have set up 'no frills' dealing services where they will carry out your buying or selling orders for the very minimum of commission, which in practice means between £10 and £30 depending largely on whether the firm is located in London or the provinces. Although commissions are no longer regulated, they seem to have settled into a norm of 1.65% of the value, subject to this minimum. If you opt for a service like this, do not expect to be able to chat to your broker about the state of the market, or whatever. At those sort of prices, they simply will not be able to afford to spend much time on small private clients. You may also find, with a basic service like this, that a broker will not accept any 'limit' orders from clients – when, for example, you instruct your broker to buy a share at 'not more than xx pence'. Unless he can execute that order immediately, he is unlikely to keep it on his books for you – again, it is simply not worth it from his point of view.

An alternative to these 'no frills dealing services', which are carried out by telephone, is to use a share shop. The first was set up in Debenhams in London a year or so ago, very much on an experimental basis, but the idea seems to be catching on with one of the clearing banks now entering the fray.

If you want more than a 'dealing only' service, plenty of brokers can offer a more rounded package, which may comprise some or all of the following but do expect to pay for these. The bigger the package, the more it is likely to cost you, whether in the form of higher commissions or an annual fee.

- advice on takeover bids and rights issues;
- portfolio valuations;
- a discretionary management service – in other words, the broker will take decisions for you, without having to consult you first;
- CGT advice;
- advice on other aspects of personal financial planning.

How do you choose the type of service you want? If you are happy to make your own decisions, a dealing only service may be right for you. If you prefer to discuss matters first, the only advice that can really be given is to 'suck it and see' – preferably go alone to meet your chosen broker, or at least talk to them over the telephone, so you can form a judgment of what they are like.

THE OTHER COSTS OF DEALING AND WHEN YOU PAY THEM

Apart from the commission to the broker, investors face other costs, including stamp duty (at $^1/_2$ per cent of the value of the shares) and VAT. Table 20 shows a few examples.

When you instruct a broker to buy some shares for you (which can be done over the telephone once your bank reference has been cleared) you may want to discuss the price with him first. Although you can look this up in the paper you should remember that what is quoted there is only the 'middle' price – to buy, the shares are likely to be more expensive (to sell, less). You can either instruct him to buy 'at best' (i.e. the best price he can obtain that day – he should be doing this anyway) or you can set limits for him, telling him not to buy unless the shares are available at (for example) 100 pence or less – though see previous comment on 'dealing only' services. Remember that if you are dealing over the telephone in this way your 'word' is also your bond; you cannot change your mind a couple of days later.

Once your order has been processed, you will receive a contract note from the broker showing the cost of the shares and all the dealing costs. All Stock Exchange transactions are carried out within an 'account period'. This is a two week period (sometimes three weeks, when bank holidays crop up) lasting from a Monday through to the Friday of the week afterwards. You have to pay within 10 days after the end of the account.

It is possible to deal 'in' the account – buy and sell within the same two week period – in which case there will be no stamp duty to pay. Commission is charged per transaction, but if you bought and sold within 'the account' there will probably be only one commission charge from the broker, not two. Another possibility is to buy shares in the last two days of an

Table 20 The costs of buying shares: examples

1 £500-worth
Stockbroker's commission*	£20.00
Plus VAT at 15%	£3.00
Stamp duty (at ½%)	£2.50
Total:	£25.50

2 £1.000-worth
Stockbroker's commission*	£20.00
Plus VAT at 15%	£3.00
Stamp duty (at ½%)	£5.00
Total:	£28.00

3 £10,000-worth
Stockbroker's commission**	£165.00
Plus VAT at 15%	£24.75
Stamp duty (at ½%)	£50.00
CSI levy	0.60
Total:	£240.35

*The minimum commission likely to be charged by a London firm of stockbrokers.

account and specify that they are to be treated as for the new account period (thus deferring your settlement date). This usually costs extra.

Once you have received the contract note and paid up, it may take several weeks before you actually receive the share certificate. Once you receive it, keep it in a safe place.

THE UK MARKET AND THE INDICES

There are three indices most commonly used to show the ups and downs of the market: the FT-All Share Index, the FT-Industrial Ordinary Index and the FT-Stock Exchange Index (abbreviated to FT-SE 100 and usually pronounced 'Footsie').

The FT-All Share is the most representative, though despite its name, it consists of only 722 shares. However, these cover 90 per cent of the market by capitalisation and the index is calculated once a day. It started in 1962.

The FT-Industrial Ordinary Index started in 1935 and it is more commonly known as the 'FT-30'. It is the most well known and arguably the least representative as it only consists of 30 shares (which are periodically reviewed). It is calculated every hour.

The FT-SE 100 is the newcomer: it started in January 1984 and it consists (with one or two exceptions) of the 100 largest companies in the market, representing 70 per cent of the market's total capitalisation. It is calculated literally minute by minute throughout the trading day. The reason this index came into existence was to enable a futures contract to be launched in equities.

In spite of the obvious drawbacks to the FT-30, people are showing as much reluctance to abandon it as they are to stop thinking in terms of feet and inches and talk about metres instead. If you ask anyone what the market is doing, the answer you will get – 'up 20 points this morning' or 'down 10' – can be taken as referring to the FT 30, whether specified or not.

The charts shown are both based on the FT-All Shares Index. The first simply shows the progress of the index over the last 15 years, the second, the index adjusted for inflation. Writing in 1987, we have had five excellent years to look back on, with the Index having more than doubled since January 1980. For most of the past year, people have been wondering 'where can we go from here?' and while it is impossible (or foolish!) to make predictions in a book where they can be proved wrong before the finished text is in the shops, the second chart might take away some of the vertigo. Adjusting for inflation over the years, the recent rise looks less alarming.

THE PLACE OF SHARES IN A PORTFOLIO

If you are going to make shares the mainstay of your portfolio, you should ideally have at least £15,000 to devote to the cause. As Table 20 shows, if you are buying shares in parcels of less than £1,000 at a time, the cost of dealing in them rises to an unacceptably high proportion of the total.

On the other hand, you have to remember that the companies you invest in can theoretically go under, so a 'spread' portfolio is essential. Ten to fifteen shares is usually held to be sufficient diversification. Any more, and you are in danger of 'diluting' the performance, any less and you will not have a reasonable spread of risk. Remember, though, that the UK stock market is only one of several possible homes for your money – there are overseas stock markets, fixed interest investments, property and so on – so your total portfolio is likely to be a good bit more than the £15,000 mentioned above.

Let us assume you are a reasonably long term 'sensible' investor – in other words, a realistic, middle-of-the-road sort of person, with no desire to indulge in out and out speculation, but, on the other hand, not the sort of person who insists on total monetary security of all his capital at every moment in time. Someone who can afford to ride out some ups and downs over the years because he can decide whether or not to cash his investments in at any point in time. In such a case, you are likely to find that a broker – or any other financial adviser, come to that – will recommend that perhaps 60 per cent to 70 per cent of your free assets should go into equity investments. But this can only be, ultimately, a matter of personal preference, as is the choice whether to buy shares direct, or go for other investment vehicles such as unit trusts or life assurance policies.

Having said you are a long term investor does not, of course, imply that you should pick 10 shares and hang on to them forever. But how do you know when, or if, to change them? If you are able to build up a good relationship with a broker, he should be supplying you with advice and maybe regular reviews of your portfolio.

Figure 3 London F.T.A. All-Share Price Index
from 1/1/70 to 12/8/87 monthly
Source: *Datastream*

If there was a secret formula that would lead to investors doing consistently better than the market average, you can be sure someone would have found it out by now – after all, they have been trying long enough! As it is, there has accumulated a sort of market lore – 'folk wisdom' if you like – which is probably as near as you will get to a secret formula and has in addition the advantage of being far more memorable and pithy than the volumes of investment analysis theories produced each year.

The first two are much the same way of saying the same thing: **'Sell too soon'** and **'Always leave some profit for the next man'**.
Psychologically, it is much harder to do than you might think; but how many investors have held on and on, hoping the shares will go even higher? And if you want any more convincing on this particular line of thought, try the French saying: **'There are more fools among buyers than sellers'**. **'Buy on the rumour, sell on the fact'** – or, as the Americans say, **'Buy on mystery, sell on history'**. This saying refers to

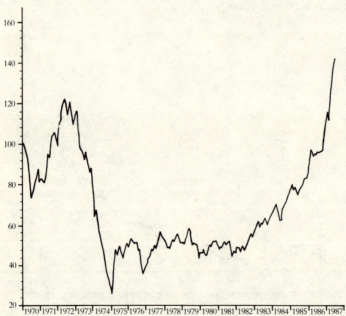

Figure 4 FT All-Share Index (adjusted for inflation)
Source: *Datastream*

the market's propensity to anticipate (and exaggerate) good news, and to overreact afterwards. A classic instance was the general election in 1979; the market surged ahead in anticipation of a Conservative victory, and when they did win, it promptly fell!

'Run your profits, cut your losses'
The first part of this almost seems to contradict the first two sayings (proverbs often do). Cutting your losses is probably as hard as leaving profits for someone else to make. It involves admitting you were wrong in the choice of a particular share; but if you hold on to a 'dud' share for years and years it is an expensive way of protecting your ego!

'Every share is attractive at a price'
The great skill here is deciding what the 'attractive' price is. People who bought Rolls Royce shares after it crashed for sixpence apiece, to paper the bathroom with the certificates, were proving this precept ultimately true; and in fact they were doubly rewarded because they eventually got back considerably more than they paid.

'Where there's a tip there's a tap'
A motto indicating the limitless cynicism of the market. It means that if a particular share is being tipped you can be sure there is someone who has a large stock of the shares in question ('on tap') they want to sell. Not necessarily true of course, but there is nothing wrong with being a little bit cynical at any rate some of the time.

And while we are on this subject, if you go in for buying share-tipping newsheets, you should be aware of the fact you are not the only one who reads them. The market makers read them too, just as they read the share tips in the weekend newspapers. This is the reason you are rarely able to buy shares the following day at the price they have been tipped at. If you intend to follow published tips in this way, it is not a bad idea to wait a few days *after* the tip has been made, in which case the share price may have settled down again.

Finally, two cautionary sayings from the other side of the Atlantic. Mark Twain once observed that October was a particularly dangerous month for speculating on the stock market. He went on to point out that **'Other dangerous** months are January, February, March, April, May, June, July, August, September, November and December'. And last of all, an American columnist known as Adam Smith wrote: **'If you don't know who you are, the Stock Market is a very expensive place to find out'.**

OTHER WAYS TO PLAY THE EQUITY MARKET

Given that a successful investor is one who can predict what is going to happen in the market, what can he do if he thinks the market, or a particular share, is going to go down rather than up? Or what if an investor feels he wants to participate in the equity market but simply does not have the £15,000-odd we recommended earlier as a sensible minimum? Or let us take a third example: a substantial investor who has built up a nice portfolio of shares that he does not want to sell – what with the selling expenses, and the CGT that will arise on disposal – yet he feels the market is going to fall in the short term. Is there anything he can do, other than grin and bear it?

The answer is yes to all three questions; and there are various ways he can go about it.

First of all, he could take out a 'Futures Contract' in the FT-SE 100 Index on LIFFE (the London International Financial Futures Exchange). Futures contracts enable you to make money whether the market is going up or down, provided you have predicted the movement correctly. This route, however, is unlikely to be of much interest to the private investor because it is very expensive.

A more rewarding route for individuals is to get to know 'Traded Options'. These are traded on the Stock Exchange, and you carry out the transaction through your broker. An option is the right to buy or sell a particular share at some specified time in the future at a fixed price. The right to buy version is called a 'call option', and the right to sell one is a 'put option'.

If you think the price of a particular share is going to go up, you take out a call option. Traded options can last, incidentally, for fixed periods of three, six or nine months but no longer. The price of the share the investor agrees on is called the 'Exercise Price': the cost of the option depends on what exercise price is chosen and the time period. Each share has a choice of several different exercise prices – the higher it is above the current price, the cheaper it will be.

Assuming the share price rises as the investor has forecast, as soon as it has passed the exercise price, he is on the way to making money. In fact the share will have to rise a bit more to take into account the cost of the option itself before he is making real money.

Once the share price has passed this point, the investor has a choice. He can either buy the shares himself at the agreed exercise price – thereby making a profit which he can realise by selling them immediately – or, remembering that we are talking about *traded* options, he can sell the option itself at a profit. Either way, he can make, in percentage terms, a much bigger profit for the amount of money he has had to 'invest' than he would if he had paid out cash for the real shares in the first place.

If an investor thinks the price of a share is going to fall, he purchases a put option, which is the right to sell shares at a fixed price. This option becomes valuable once the price falls below the exercise price (it is valuable to holders of those shares, as they could get a better than market price for them if they had that option – alternatively, the investor could buy the shares at the (lower) market price, and sell them at his (higher) exercise price). Again, there will be a range of exercise prices to choose from, and here, exactly contrary to call options, the *lower* the exercise price is, in relation to the current price, the cheaper it will be.

Obviously, for every call or put option an investor takes out, there has to be someone, somewhere in the market who takes an opposite view, and who thinks *he* is going to be the one who makes money by taking your option premiums, while you will not actually exercise your option because the price will not move the way you expect. 'Writers' of options are usually institutional investors.

Before the traded options market came into being in 1978, there were conventional options, which may still be bought. These last for three months (sometimes you can arrange one month options) and like traded options, are organised through your stockbroker. The major, obvious, difference between the two is that conventional options cannot be traded – they are either exercised or lapse.

The beauty of traded options are three-fold:
1 They are cheap compared to buying the shares themselves.
2 Your opportunity for profits is increased, while the potential for loss is limited to the cost of the option.
3 Profits are subject to CGT not income tax.

Traded options are available in about 20 leading shares (including companies like Marks & Spencer, GEC, ICI and Lonrho). Since May 1985, you can effectively take out options on the market itself, for which purpose the FT-SE 100 index is used.

A third alternative is to gamble – seriously. There are several organisations that take bets on such things as the level of the FT-SE 100 Index. They work in a similar fashion to traded options, except that you deal directly with the organisation concerned, not with a stockbroker. The main difference as far as the investor is concerned is that any proceeds are effectively tax-free. Technically, the bets are subject to betting tax but this is borne by the company itself and is included in the 'spreads' they quote. The other point to watch is that losses are not automatically limited – you have to take action to 'close' your bet if the price movement is going against you.

OTHER TYPES OF SHARE

We have only been talking about ordinary shares so far, but there are other types of share, and other securities issued by companies that you may come across.

Preference shares are fixed interest shares whose holders are entitled to a fixed dividend each year. They are usually 'cumulative' shares in the sense that if the company passes the dividend one year, it is bound to make it up the next (there is no such right for ordinary shares). They are theoretically marginally safer than ordinary shares in that on liquidation, preference shareholders stand in front of ordinary shareholders for any proceeds available from the company. But to a private investor, preference shares on the whole offer a rather unattractive combination of risk (as with any equity investment) plus limited rewards.

Convertibles are loan stock issued by a company which carry with them the right to 'convert' into ordinary shares at a predetermined price during a fixed term in the future. A much nicer animal than the 'pref'; here you get the security of fixed income plus the possibility of rewards on conversion.

Debentures are loan stock that is 'secured' on the assets of a company. They are thus relatively secure fixed-interest vehicles, offering yields only fractionally above gilt-edged stock. One step down the security ladder is *unsecured loan stock*, offering yields a touch higher. Take advice before investing in any of these.

THE MENAGERIE OF THE STOCK MARKET

Many of the terms used in the stock market will be familiar to readers, but we have rounded up some of the most common terms.

Bear (adjective, bearish): a pessimist – hence 'a bear market'.

Blue chips: blue chips were the highest value gambling chips, hence the biggest, most secure companies.

Bull (adjective, bullish): optimist, someone who thinks the market is going up. Hence 'a bull market', where the market has risen strongly.

Contango: if you buy some shares intending to make a profit by dealing in the account (i.e. sell them again in the same two week period so you do not actually have to pay), but then the price of the share does not move upwards the way you expect, you can ask your broker to arrange 'a contango' in other words, carry it forward to the next account period.

OTC: the letters here stand for 'Over the Counter'. A small market in the UK but massive in the States, where 15,000 stocks are traded 'over the counter'. In fact, is it not a formal market at all. Various licensed dealers are prepared to 'make a market' in these shares (in other words, they act as jobbers as well as brokers). There are no regulations as such; it has to be a case of 'let the potential buyer beware'.

'Rule 163(2)': before the USM came into existence, this type of company was often traded under the Stock Exchange rule number 163(2); a rule which allowed occasional transactions in unlisted shares. There are far less regulations involved here and it was because this route was becoming so popular that the Stock Exchange decided to set up the USM.

Stag: 'stagging' a new issue involves applying for masses of shares (more than you want for yourself) at the fixed issue price. You do it because you think that when dealing opens, it will be at a 'premium' (i.e. higher than the fixed price) so you will be able to make a quick profit by selling your suplus before you have actually had to pay for them.

Unlike the 'bull' and 'bear', the derivation of 'stag' is known; it comes from a street in the City of London, called Stag Alley (now known as Capel Court) where people queued up to lodge their applications for the shares of new railway companies – all the rage in those days.

USM, OTC, 163(2): this bunch of hieroglyphics refers to the various 'markets' on which shares that are not listed can be traded. The most formal is the Unlisted Securities Market (USM) which started life in November 1980 under the auspices of the Stock Exchange.

It is basically a 'second tier' market for small, fast expanding companies (e.g. Body Shop and the Miss World Group) who do not want to go to the trouble and expense of seeking a full listing. Such companies still have to comply with a great many regulations before they can be quoted on the USM. One attraction for small companies though is that only 10 per cent of their capital need be in public hands compared to the 25 per cent of fully listed companies. There are now well over 300 companies on the USM and to buy or sell these shares, simply go via your broker. There is now the 3rd market as well (see page 53).

PERSONAL EQUITY PLANS (PEPS)

As from the beginning of 1987, investors have been able to put a limited sum (currently £2,400 a year) into a Personal Equity Plan. Providing the investment is held until the end of the calendar year following the year of investment, profits are free of Capital Gains Tax, and dividends of Income Tax (as long as they're re-invested in the plan, not drawn out).

Many banks, unit trust and life companies run 'packaged' Peps with a spread of shares chosen by the managers. So also do some stockbrokers, but by no means all.

Although the amount of money that can be invested is small, and the effective tax breaks minimal – given that few people pay CGT anyway, and the yield on a £2,400 investment is likely to be less than £100 a year – it's still worth taking out such a plan if it fits in with your existing investment plans.

Some stockbrokers, while not promoting a packaged plan to the public, will arrange a Pep for their private clients, tailored to their particular needs. If you don't have that sort of relationship with a broker, and are looking at the various packaged plans available, the things to look out for include:

1 the level of charges (some are quite high)
2 the spread of shares in the plan
3 the character of the portfolio.

Some groups run several different portfolios – some high risk, some conservatively managed, investing predominantly in blue chips.

A unit trust can also be used for a Pep but only for a maximum of £420 a year or (if greater) 25% of the total invested.

WHERE TO FIND OUT MORE

The stock exchange publishes a mass of useful (free) booklets including *An Introduction to Buying and Selling Shares, The Stock Exchange, The Gilt-Edged Market, A Simple Guide to Traded Options*. The Stock Exchange, London EC2N 1HP, 01-588 2355.

For further more detailed reading, try *The Stock Market: A Guide for the Private Investor,* by Neil Stapley, published by Woodhead Faulkner.

In September, Telegraph Publications released the title, *Stocks and Shares,* written by the former city editor of *Financial Weekly,* Roger Hardman.

Traded Options

THE COURSE FOR THE PRIVATE INVESTOR

Traded options are the most exciting investment opportunity in the City today. Spectacular profits are regularly available — not just to the professionals, but to anyone with the expertise a specialist market demands.

The City Investment School offers an inexpensive but comprehensive home learning programme enabling you to deal successfully in the fastest-growing market in the London Stock Exchange.

- ★ **Twelve written lectures** prepared by experts and forwarded to you at weekly intervals
- ★ **Simulated trading** using our computerised link to the Stock Exchange, allowing you to gain invaluable practical experience — risk-free!
- ★ **Regular personal assessments** by experienced investment analysts
- ★ **An exclusive fortnightly Newsletter** and Stock Market update
- ★ **A software package** to boost your investment analysis
- ★ **Your own individual tutor** always available for consultation

For full details, ring 01-353 9365 or return the coupon below

----

CITY INVESTMENT SCHOOL, 11 Bolt Court, Fleet Street, London EC4A 3DQ

Full name (Mr/Mrs/Ms)...

Address ....

................................Postcode..............................

Telephone ....

TT 30/7/98

CHAPTER 6

UNIT TRUSTS AND OFFSHORE FUNDS (I)

Unit trusts, offshore funds and the investment vehicles described in succeeding chapters, investment trusts and life assurance products all have a common thread running through them. The most elegant description of their basic reason for existence is to be found in the prospectus for the very first investment trust, founded in 1868. So although it is slightly out of context, it is not out of date and it is not inappropriate to quote it here.

> We intend to provide the investor of moderate means the same advantage as the large capitalists in diminishing risk . . . by spreading the investment over a number of stocks.

In other words, to provide a spread of risk. Other advantages may emerge throughout the next few chapters like active investment management, possible tax advantages, or easy access to overseas markets. First and foremost, however, a unit trust (and its competitors) exists to give the investor a spread of risk over a number of shares and/or other securities that he could not possibly achieve on his own without considerable sums of money to do so.

As we mentioned in the last chapter, a 'sensible' amount to consider investing directly into the UK equity market is likely to be £15,000 at the very least – and such is the range and extent of unit trusts these days that many investors with £40,000 or £50,000 to their credit find the choice offered by these 'collective' investments so wide that they have no need to venture out into direct holdings.

There are over 120 unit trust management companies, managing around £40 billion of investors' money between them. The top 20 groups, who account for just over £22 billion of the total, are shown in Table 21. Most companies are members of the Unit Trust Association, which supplies a booklet giving details of members' names and addresses free of charge.

Table 21 Top 20 unit trust groups

Group	Funds under management* £m
M & G	2,771.0
Allied Dunbar	2,142.6
Save & Prosper	2,000.2
Standard	1,942.5
Henderson	1,757.2
Barclays Unicorn	1,490.2
TSB Unit Trusts	1,201.3
NM Schroder	1,179.2
Mercury	952.9
MIM Britannia	952.1
Hill Samuel	810.3
Abbey	715.7
Prudential	682.8
Fidelity	647.6
Target	547.7
Prolific	502.1
Legal & General	484.3
GT	461.5
Barrington	458.6
Framlington	453.9

* End 1986.
Source: *Unit Trust Yearbook*.

There are now more than a thousand different unit trusts ranging across the whole investment spectrum from general UK funds to specialist funds such as Japanese Smaller Company trusts or Preference Share trusts. We look in detail at the investment choice in the next chapter.

WHAT IS A UNIT TRUST?

A unit trust is a trust. You might think this does not need saying – but investment trusts, for instance, are not. The money and the investments are all held by the trustees (usually one of the big banks or insurance companies) on behalf of the unit holders, and part of the trustees' job is to make sure that the managers fulfil the terms of the trust deed. This deed will set out what the objectives of the trust are, how the money must be invested, what the charges are, how the price of the units is calculated and so on.

Unit trusts are regulated ultimately by the Department of Trade and Industry (DTI) which itself lays down what a trust may invest in. The general rule is any quoted Stock Exchange security, meaning shares and gilts; they can also invest up to 25 per cent of their portfolio in unlisted securities, meaning, generally, in shares on the USM although up to 5 per cent can be in OTC or 'unquoted' stocks. Recently, the rules were relaxed to allow managers to make use of traded options in a limited way, but as yet relatively few trusts have trust deeds which enable them to do this.

Another DTI ruling is concerned to ensure that there is an adequate spread of risk: no more than 5 per cent (normally) of the total portfolio can be invested in any one company's shares. This means the lowest number of shares you can have in a unit trust is 20; in fact, most trusts run portfolios with between 50 and 100 different shares. This ruling can be relaxed in special circumstances to 7.5 per cent, and the managers are also usually given a fair bit of time to adjust their portfolio if one of their choices has proved so successful that the price zooms up to bring their holding above the limit.

There is another rule trust managers have to obey, which is similar to that above, only 'inside out'. Trusts cannot acquire more than 10 per cent of the issued share capital of any one company. The reason for this is that trusts should not be going about building up controlling stakes in companies – that is not what they are here for – though this rule really falls flat on its face where groups have a large number of trusts, in which case they could easily build up large stakes in a company without infringing the letter of the law.

The Department is currently in the throes of finalising a new set of rules which are expected to allow new types of unit trust investing in property, commodities and bank deposits as well as shares and gilts. The new rules should be in place by the end of 1987.

CHARGES

There are two types of charge levied by unit trust managers. The first, the initial charge, is taken off the investment right at the beginning. These days, the typical initial charge, especially on recently created trusts is 5 per cent; some of the older ones are still at 3.5 per cent or 4 per cent, while some of the new specialist overseas trusts have charges of 5.5 or even 6 per cent. The level of the charges will be specified in the trust deed. Sometimes managers will stipulate a much higher initial charge in the trust deed – in one recent case it was actually 10 per cent – even though they do not intend to levy it in the forseeable future. They do this simply to avoid the bother of going back to their unit holders at a later date in order to get permission to increase it.

Managers can also make a 'rounding up' charge which is added to the initial charge, to avoid unit prices being quoted in tiny fractions. The rounding is limited to 1.25 pence or 1 per cent, whichever is the smaller.

Out of this initial charge, the managers pay commission to intermediaries who sell the trusts for them. The 'basic' commission is 1.25 per cent, but to this can be added a 'marketing allowance' of another 1.75 per cent, bringing the total up to 3 per cent. The balance goes towards the managers' costs, including advertising.

If investors buy their units direct from the managers rather than through an intermediary, they do not themselves benefit from that extra 3 per cent, which is simply retained by the managers. Sometimes though, particularly if a new trust is being launched through direct advertising, the managers will have an 'opening offer' lasting for a month or so, during which investors get a 1 per cent discount off the offer price.

Secondly there is the annual charge, amounting generally to between 0.5 per cent and 1 per cent. Again, it is the older established trusts which tend to have the lower charge, and again, there has been a tendency for the annual charge to rise. Some of the new overseas trusts have annual charges of up to 1.5 per cent.

Obviously, all other things being equal, it is preferable to go for a trust which has lower charges, but one should not lose sight of the wood for the trees here. The difference in performance can be vast – as the figures in the next chapter show – so much so that an extra 1 per cent a year pales into insignificance.

One point to watch out for, if you intend to be an active investor in trusts, moving from one to another, is whether the groups concerned offer any discounts when you switch between one trust and another, or whether you are forced to pay the 'entrance fee' in full every time you move. It seems to be a growing practice among groups to offer such discounts – it is to their own advantage, after all, to encourage you to keep your money within their group, even if you decide to alter the investment emphasis. In one case at least, the managers offer a

4 per 'discount' which means you are scarcely penalised at all for switching trusts.

BID AND OFFER

Having said that the initial charge is generally 5 per cent, if you look in the papers at unit trust prices you will see that the difference between the two prices quoted there is always more than this percentage. The 'bid' (what you get when you sell your units) and 'offer' (what you pay) prices are calculated according to rules laid down by the DTI and they include rather more than the initial charge.

The full offer price that the managers can charge takes into account not just the value of the shares in the portfolio (which are valued at their offer price, i.e., the price at which the trust could buy those shares in the market that day) but also the stockbrokers' commission, stamp duty, and various other items such as unit trust instrument duty. Then there is the value of any uninvested cash in the fund, plus any dividends or other interest received or accrued. To all of this is added the manager's initial charge of (say) 5 per cent plus rounding.

The full bid price takes account of the *bid* value of the shares in the portfolio, less selling expenses, together with uninvested cash etc., and a rounding down adjustment. An example of this is shown in Table 22.

The difference between 'full' offer and 'full' bid when you take all these extra items into account can be as much as 11 per cent. However, not many people would be prepared to buy an investment that would have to show a gain of 11 per cent before they started to make any profits at all, and in fact what the managers do is operate on a much narrower 'spread' than the legal maximum allowed. The typical spread is around 6 per cent. This 'spread' can be set anywhere on the range between full offer and full bid. If a trust is expanding, meaning new money is coming in and the managers are having to go out and buy more shares, the spread will be set at the higher end of the spectrum, in which case it is said to be on an 'offer basis'.

If the trust is contracting, on the other hand, meaning the managers are having to sell off shares to meet the redemptions, the trust is likely to be on a 'bid' basis. In other words, the bid price will be at the lowest permitted by the DTI regulations, with the offer price set around 6 per cent above that. In the

Table 22 Bid and offer price calculations

Offer price calculations	p
Value of securities in the fund at lowest market dealing offer price	£5,000,000
On 10m units, this represents a value of securities per unit of	50,000
Add stamp duty (0.5%)	0.250
Add brokerage (0.25%)	0.125
Add unit trust instrument duty (0.25%)	0.125
	50.500
Add accrued income (£60,000)	0.600
	51.100
Add initial charge (5%)	2.555
	53.655
Add rounding	0.445
Offer price per unit	54.100

Bid price calculation	p
Value of securities in fund at highest market dealing bid prices	£4,900,000.
On 10m units this represents a value of securities per unit of	49.000
Subtract brokerage (0.25%)	0.123
	48.877
Add accrued income (£60,000)	0.600
	49.477
Subtract rounding	0.477
Bid price per unit	49.000

Source: *Unit Trust Yearbook*

majority of cases, trusts will be on an offer basis, meaning that unitholders who are cashing in their units are strictly speaking getting more than they are entitled to. But as long as you buy and sell on the same basis, then whichever it is makes little difference to the result.

Managers do not like to move sharply from a full offer to full bid basis; the abrupt change of some 6 per cent in unit prices would not be welcomed by investors. If they decide it would be prudent to move down from an offer towards a bid basis (perhaps because markets are falling and they expect large numbers of units will be cashed in) then they will usually try to do so slowly over a period of a week or more.

Some of the very old, very big unit trusts (some are 40 years old or more) are permanently on a bid basis, often simply because the original generation of unitholders is dying off and their holdings being liquidated, without any new money flowing in.

DIFFERENT TYPES OF UNIT

Some trusts aim to provide capital growth, others income, or a balance between income and growth. The capital growth orientated trusts will generally have a very low yield – perhaps under 1 per cent – and in this case it is pointless for the unitholder, and a needless expense for the managers, to have tiny amounts of income paid out twice a year.

Some trusts have 'accumulation' units, meaning that any income received is simply ploughed back into the fund, and the unit price will rise accordingly. Accumulation units do not mean that the unitholder escapes liability to income tax on them; he will still have to declare it (the managers send him the information).

With income on more general trusts, one of the main purposes of holding the trust is to receive income, so these trusts have 'distribution' or 'income' units, which in most cases means income is distributed, net of basic rate tax, twice a year. Some trusts distribute quarterly, a few monthly.

Many trusts have a choice of unit, distribution or accumulation; the choice depends solely on whether you want to receive the income or not. Some trusts will offer to reinvest your income rather than offer accumulation units. This is not such a good deal, as it means investors have to pay the initial charge on the money that is reinvested.

The first distribution a unitholder receives from his trust may include an amount known as an 'equalisation payment'. This is a method of dealing with the fact that only part of the income that has accrued to the trust since the last distribution date relates to the time the investor has held the units – however, he has effectively paid for the rest of the income as it will have been included in the offer price he paid. So the distribution received is partly 'income' and partly a repayment of a portion of that capital. This is the 'equalisation' payment: for tax purposes, it does not count as income, but you have to deduct it from the original purchase price paid for CGT purposes.

FUNDS OF FUNDS

In the last couple of years, a new type of unit trust has made its appearance – a 'fund of funds' or 'managed fund'. Three or four groups have now launched a product along these lines. Essentially, it is a 'super trust' that invests in the group's range of other specialist trusts, changing the investment emphasis as market conditions dictate.

The concept has attracted widespread comment, its supporters as vociferous as its detractors. On the plus side, it has been pointed out that small investors should not opt for ultra-specialist funds as they would find it very hard to know when or if to switch from market to market, and that the product itself actually mirrors the way that investment management works. You need one investment specialist who concentrates on particular markets, with another prepared to take an overview, deciding which markets overall provide the best prospects.

The critics accept that there is nothing inherently nasty about this new product, for instance there are no hidden double charges. But they question why it is necessary to have a separate vehicle to achieve this aim: what is wrong with an ordinary international trust? Because there are, at least potentially, disadvantages with the fund of funds arrangement. The fund of funds over-manager may decide, for example, to pull out of Japan. That may be all right for his unitholders, but what about those who have decided to invest directly in the underlying specialist Japanese trust? If this trust is suddenly losing a large part of its money under management, will this not make life extra hard for the Japanese fund manager, who may be forced to realise some investment he does not want to, just to meet the dictates of the fund of funds man?

In practice, it will not work like that, say the funds of funds supporters. Anyway, the total amount invested in the fund of funds (each group, incidentally, is only allowed one such vehicle) is unlikely to be that significant compared to the underlying trusts.

I remain fairly neutral on the subject. The proof of the pudding will be in the investment performance, and it is too soon to tell. If funds of funds regularly outperform the ordinary international trusts, they may be worth looking at. But there are some good, long-term performance records from ordinary international trusts (though not necessarily from those groups which have espoused the fund of funds concept). We will have to wait and see.

UNIT TRUSTS AND TAX
INCOME TAX

If the income consists of dividends from UK shares or interest from UK gilts, the unit trust itself has no liability to tax. The responsibility for paying tax passes straight to the unitholder. Basic rate taxpayers need take no further action, as dividends are paid (or reinvested) net of basic rate tax; non-taxpayers may reclaim the tax paid, while higher rate taxpayers face a further charge.

Income from other sources, e.g. deposit interest, dividends from overseas shares and so on, is liable to tax in the trust at corporation tax rates (which for the 1987/8 tax year is 35 per cent). Once again, higher rate taxpayers may face a further tax charge.

CAPITAL GAINS TAX

Any liability to CGT is the unitholder's, not the trust's. The trust itself is not liable to CGT on its dealings. This means that profits of up to £6,600 in the 1987/8 tax year may be realised before tax is payable. All the investor's gains, not just those relating to unit trusts sales, are combined together for this purpose.

SPECIAL FACILITIES FOR THE INVESTOR

Share exchange schemes
Unit trust groups run various schemes designed to encourage investors to buy their units. Most groups offer 'share exchange schemes' for individuals who want to realise direct holdings of equities to invest in unit trusts. There will always be a cost advantage to the investor. If the managers want your shares for their own trusts, they may pay you the offer price for the shares, rather than the bid price less the selling expenses you would incur if you sold privately: if not, you will receive the bid price, but the group will often pay the selling expenses themselves.

Regular savings schemes and additional investments

The minimum lump sum investment in a unit trust these days is typically £500 or £1,000. But there is an alternative. Many groups run regular savings schemes designed to encourage the small investor to get a taste for, and to build up a holding in, unit trusts. The schemes generally stipulate a minimum monthly saving of £20 or more, though there are usually no penalties if you want to stop and/or withdraw the cash at any time. In most cases there is no additional charge for investing in this way, though this is a point to watch out for. Income is not distributed if units are bought in this way as it would be too complicated to administer. Plans which offer accumulation units rather than reinvestment of income provide a better deal.

Most groups also allow existing unitholders to add to their holding in any trust at any time. The minimum investment is usually much smaller than the original lump sum requirement – perhaps £100.

Why save regularly?

To digress slightly here, it is worth pointing out a possible advantage to building up a unit trust holding this way, by investing regularly rather than in one lump sum. You benefit from an arithmetical effect known as 'Pound Cost Averaging'. If unit prices fall, your money will buy a greater number of units, the net effect being that at the end of any given period, the average cost of the units you have bought is less than their average price over the period. A simple example (using exaggerated price movements to make the point) is shown in Table 23.

The real benefit of pound cost averaging is to do with timing. By saving regularly, you are committing yourself to buying units at times when the price has slumped, which is psychologically rather hard but is, of course, the advantageous time to do it.

Schemes for a regular income

Monthly income schemes are available from many groups. Since most trusts pay out dividends twice a year, this means investors will need a holding of six different trusts, with different distribution dates, to achieve a pay out twelve times a year. The larger groups have a range of different income trusts (for more details, see the next chapter) and can put together a 'package' in this way.

Table 23 Pound cost averaging

Month of purchase	Unit price	Number of units bought for £20
1	50p	40
2	30p	66
3	20p	100
4	40p	50
5	60p	34
6	80p	24
Average price	46.7p	314 units bought for £120 average price paid: 38.2p

It is also possible to make up your own package using trusts of different groups, which may be preferable. The schemes run by individual groups generally include a gilts or fixed interest trust which, while providing a high initial income, offers little scope for a *rising* income which is the most important point about these schemes. A few groups have trusts which pay income every month – most do not, as this requirement will inevitably place constraints on the investment policy.

An alternative is a 'Withdrawal Scheme'. What happens here is that a certain number of units are automatically cashed in for you to receive a regular 'income'. These schemes can be dangerous in a falling market if you have elected to take a fixed sum rather than a fixed number of units. If prices fall, the number of units that will have to be cashed in to provide the fixed sum will rise – and you could find, in an unnervingly short time, that you have eaten away most of your capital as 'income'. That said, a withdrawal scheme can be tax effective, particularly for higher rate taxpayers, simply because much of the 'income' is in fact capital and therefore liable only to CGT – and by utilising the annual exemption, it can mean effectively a tax-free 'income'. Even for such people, however, an automatic withdrawal scheme is dangerous – far better to keep control over it and encash units only when the price has risen.

KEEPING TRACK OF YOUR INVESTMENT

Managers generally revalue daily, and prices are quoted in

both the *Financial Times* and *The Daily Telegraph*. This means you can monitor your investment on a regular basis. If you are thinking of selling, remember it is the lower of the two prices, the bid price, which is relevant. If you have a large investment in a trust – say £20,000 or more – it is possible that you will be quoted a different price to that published though this normally only happens where professional advisers are dealing on behalf of a number of investors and the total amount is considerable.

Apart from following the price record, and reading any relevant articles in the personal finance sections of newspapers, investors have the Managers' Report to consult. This is usually sent with the distributions twice a year, an annual or final report and an interim (half yearly) report.

Reports have to contain certain information such as details of the managers, the trustees, and the auditors; there will be a commentary on the investment performance of the fund and the background to it; details of the portfolio as at the distribution date, and changes made since the last report and income and capital accounts. The reports can be useful in assessing the progress of your investments – though the information concerned is inevitably out of date – and also of the managers' investment strategy. See the next chapter.

HOW TO INVEST

Investors can deal direct with the unit trust group, either by phone or letter or, for example, using the coupon form from an advertisement; or they can arrange their investments through an intermediary such as a stockbroker, bank or other professional adviser.

In all cases, investors receive a contract note initially, giving details of the transaction, which is followed around a month later by the Unit Certificate itself. To sell, unitholders have to send their certificate back to the group. It usually takes two or three days to get a cheque back from a sale.

OFFSHORE FUNDS

Offshore funds are in many respects similar to unit trusts, offering private investors a spread of risk and professional management in return for a fee in the shape of charges. They are all based 'offshore' i.e. outside the United Kingdom mainland: Jersey, Guernsey and the Isle of Man are popular homes, as well as more exotic places like Bermuda, the Cayman Islands and the Netherlands Antilles. 'Offshore', however, can also mean places such as Luxembourg and Switzerland.

As far as the UK-based investor is concerned, there are only limited motives for investing in them: offshore funds are primarily aimed at the non-resident individual (UK expatriates, American expatriates, etc.) who might gain tax advantages by investing in a fund in a low tax area, as most offshore funds are, outside his home country.

Offshore funds can take various forms: they can be investment trusts, unit trusts or open-ended investment companies which have the power to issue and redeem their own shares. The exact legal framework will differ according to the country in which the fund is based. The prospectus will give details.

Why should a UK-based investor bother with offshore funds? There are three possible answers; but there are some drawbacks as well.

WHAT ARE THE ADVANTAGES AND DISADVANTAGES?

Investment flexibility
Offshore funds are not limited in the way that UK unit trusts are as to what they may invest in. For example, an offshore commodity fund may invest, not just in the shares of commodity companies (as UK unit trusts are obliged to do) but in commodities themselves, or commodity futures. Currency funds, which aim to make profits by taking advantage of movements in exchange rates, are all based offshore. Offshore funds are not bound by the same regulations regarding spread of risk or unlisted securities as applies to their onshore counterparts.

Taxation
Offshore funds do not enable UK investors to escape UK tax, but in some circumstances there can be advantages to investing in this way. All offshore funds must, for UK tax purposes, be one of two types: either 'Distributor' or 'Accumulator' funds. Funds which distribute at least 85 per cent of their income will normally qualify for 'Distributor' status (this is granted by the Inland Revenue retrospectively). UK investors receive their income gross and pay tax on it in the usual way, while any

capital gains they make are liable to CGT when realised.

'Accumulator' funds roll-up their income. This means that UK investors are not liable to income tax at the time the income is ploughed back into the fund, but when the shares are finally sold, *all* the profits, whether they came from income or capital growth, are liable to income tax.

How this affects individual investors depends very much both on their personal circumstances and the nature of the fund. A fund that invests, for example, in sterling bank deposits and other money market instruments will never have any capital gains. So if a UK investor chooses a fund that rolls up its income, he can defer his income tax charge until he actually withdraws his money from the fund (by which time, he could be in a lower tax bracket than at present); and if he wants a regular income from such a fund, he can cash in a number of the shares equal to the amount of income the fund had produced. He will have to pay some income tax, but not that much: because he is cashing in shares, some of the money he is receiving is technically part of his 'capital', and thus not liable to income tax.

Disadvantages
The first point to be made about offshore funds is that because they are not subject to UK regulations, the investor is not as well protected as he would be investing in a UK-based fund. This need be only a theoretical disadvantage if he invests with well known groups which are subsidiaries or associated companies of respectable UK institutions, but not all offshore funds are run by such groups.

The second disadvantage is that charges are generally higher, although this is partly offset by the fact that offshore funds are not liable to UK stamp duty on purchases of shares. The initial charge may be no higher than a UK trust's charge – indeed, the 'spread' between bid and offer price may be narrower because of the absence of stamp duty; however, the usual practice is to charge the fund on an annual basis for such items as custodian or trustee's and auditor's fees in addition to an annual management charge (with a unit trust, all expenses are met out of the annual charge), while in the case of a recently launched fund, the setting-up expenses are usually reimbursed out of the fund over a number of years.

Finally, if you are investing in a fund that is aiming for all-out capital growth, it is vital from your point of view that the fund gets, and keeps, distributor status. If it lost it in the year you cashed your units in, you would have an income tax bill to pay on all the profits made. The main criterion for achieving distributor status is, as mentioned, that the fund distributes at least 85% of its income. But that is not the only one; the DTI can refuse to grant distributor status if it decides the fund has been 'trading' rather than 'investing' – a pretty nebulous concept which can mean simply a fund with active or aggressive investment management. One or two funds have been caught out in this respect in the past and denied distributor status even though they have carefully paid out all their income.

To make matters worse, distributor status is always granted retrospectively, a year at a time in arrears, so investors can never know for sure that they will be out of the woods until after the event.

UMBRELLA FUNDS

A fairly recent development in the offshore fund field, which has been designed with the circumstances of UK investors in mind, are 'umbrella funds'. With UK unit trusts, every time an investor wants to switch his portfolio from one investment sector to another, he is liable to capital gains tax on the profits made. Offshore umbrella funds will have a range of specialist sub-funds within a single overall fund, and, under current rules at any rate, investors can switch between them without incurring CGT until the shares themselves are sold.

HOW TO INVEST

Offshore funds cannot use 'money off the page' advertisements in UK newspapers in the way unit trusts can. They may advertise their funds indirectly by offering readers a copy of their prospectus.

Individuals who want to invest should usually go via their professional adviser.

Prices of offshore funds are quoted in the *Financial Times*.

WHERE TO FIND OUT MORE

The Unit Trust Association publishes a free booklet called *Explaining Unit Trusts*. They also produce general performance statistics (see the next chapter). They do not, however, give advice or recommendations about investment sectors or particular groups. Most of the groups themselves also produce numerous booklets, brochures, etc. describing their range of trusts.

The *Unit Trust Yearbook* is published once a year by FT Business Publishing. It contains details of all unit trusts available and of the groups themselves. For more general background reading, try *Unit Trusts: What Every Investor Should Know* by Christopher Gilchrist published by Woodhead Faulkner.

Unit Trust Association
Park House
16 Finsbury Circus
London EC2M 7JP

CHAPTER 7

UNIT TRUSTS AND OFFSHORE FUNDS (II): THE INVESTMENT CHOICE

With more than a thousand different trusts on the menu, it is not particularly easy to know where to start ordering. The number of trusts has been growing by leaps and bounds over the last few years, as Table 24 shows. Many trusts will have similar aims and specialisations, and there are really two basic choices for the investor to make: one, the management group and two, the type of trust most suited to his needs.

The Unit Trust Association divides trusts for the purposes of performance comparisons into 18 different sectors, but the most basic categorisation boils down to four different types.
1 Trusts aiming primarily to provide the investor with income.
2 Trusts offering a balance between growth and income.

Table 24 Authorised unit trusts

Year	Number
1976	352
1977	393
1978	421
1979	459
1980	493
1981	529
1982	553
1983	630
1984	687
1985	806
1986	964
1987 (end June)	1,049

Source: *Unit Trust Association*

3 Trusts concentrating on capital growth, perhaps by investing in a particular sector of the market such as smaller companies.
4 Trusts investing overseas.

The fourth category is really a subsection of the third, as by far the majority of overseas-invested trusts aim to provide capital growth rather than income. The reason behind this is largely based on taxation considerations. Until recently, unit trusts were at a disadvantage as concerned providing income from overseas sources. But now that corporation tax rates are being reduced, a number of international trusts aiming to provide an income have been launched, and their number is likely to increase.

The 18 categories used by the UTA break these basic categories down further, enabling detailed performance comparisons to be made. The sectors are as follows.

UK general
Funds invested in the UK market aiming to provide a balanced mix of income and growth. To qualify for this category, the yield must be within 25 per cent (either way) of that on the FT-All Share Index, and at least 75 per cent of the portfolio must be in UK equities (some of these 'general' funds will also have overseas holdings).

UK growth
Trusts invested primarily in UK equities (with 75 per cent being the minimum again) aiming to provide capital growth rather than income and with a yield at least 25 per cent below the yield on the FT-All Share Index. This sector includes some specialist growth trusts such as those investing in smaller companies, special situations and so on.

UK equity income
Trusts aiming to provide an above average income from investments primarily in UK equities. The yield should be at least 25 per cent above the FT-All Share Index.

Mixed income
Again, trusts aiming to provide an income, but which include investments in preference shares and other fixed interest securities, as well as equities. Here, the yield is generally around a third higher than the FT-All Share Index.

Gilt and fixed interest income
Trusts invested in UK gilts and other fixed interest securities, with an income objective. The yardstick used here is that the yield should be at least 75 per cent of War Loan stock.

Gilt and fixed interest growth
Trusts aiming to provide capital growth from investments in

gilts, etc. The remaining sectors are all concerned primarily with producing capital growth.

Investment Trust units
For investors who are attracted by the idea of investment trusts (see next chapter) and who would like a spread of risk.

Financial and property shares
'Financial' meaning insurance companies, banks, etc.

Commodity and energy shares
Including gold share trusts.

International
The most general of overseas-invested trusts, investing in all the major markets of the world. Some trusts in this category will keep an almost permanent split between the different markets (e.g. they will always have at least 40 per cent of the trust invested in the US, at least 20 per cent in Japan and so on; others will be much more active, 'market hopping' in pursuit of higher returns).

International income
These trusts form a separate category and comprise all overseas-invested trusts (whether international or concentrating on a particular market, such as the US or Europe) which aim to provide the investor with a relatively high level of income as well as capital growth.

Managed funds
These are otherwise known as 'funds of funds' (see page 82) and form a category of their own.

Then there are trusts investing in specific markets, where at least 85 per cent of the portfolio is expected to be in equities of that market. These are:

North America
Europe
Australia
Japan
Far East –meaning those trusts which do not specifically concentrate on one particular market (e.g. Japan) but invest in the

other Far Eastern markets as well, such as Hong Kong, Singapore and Malaysia and Australia. In this sector come the handful of specialist trusts which concentrate exclusively on Hong Kong or on Singapore and Malaysia.

Finally, there are *exempt trusts;* not of interest to the individual investor directly, as they are set up for pension funds and charities to invest in.

Table 25 Past performance: growth unit trusts

Sector	Results of £1,000 investment . . . years ago in median fund		
	5	10	15
UK Growth	4,241	8,540	7,839
International	3,275	5,338	5,393
Far East	3,694	6,139	—
Japan	5,159	9,332	11,497
Australia	2,457	3,687	3,316
North America	2,642	4,045	3,977
Europe	4,534	9,672	6,884
Commodity & Energy	2,325	4,306	5,367
Investment Trust units	3,891	8,239	8,028
Financial & Property	4,613	8,812	7,534
Building society	1,539	2,108	2,957
FT-All Share Index (income reinvested)	5,178	8,639	9,643

Note: A gap indicates that no trusts have been in existence that long. All figures include net reinvested income, offer to bid basis. Information as at 1 July 1987.
Source: *Unit Trust Association.*

Although comparisons of past performance can be misleading, particularly if they are used as a sort of reverse crystal ball to try to predict what is going to happen in the future, it is interesting to see how these sectors have fared in relation to each other in the past. Table 25 shows the results of a £1,000 investment for the various growth categories.

These figures, produced by the Unit Trust Association, take the 'median' trust in each category, meaning the middle one rather than the average. For comparison purposes, the results of an identical investment in a building society account is shown, and the theroetical result of investing £1,000 into the FT-All Share Index over the same periods.

'Index Comparisons' should be treated with caution. Although managers frequently use them in their advertisements (when the result is in their favour, naturally) the fact is that if the investment portfolio of a trust performed exactly in line with the index, the net result would be significantly lower, because index figures do not take into account the costs of buying and selling shares, nor do they have charges (initial and annual) to take into account. And if you are using an index to judge the result of an overseas fund, remember that indices take no account of currency movements, which for a unit trust whose results are expressed in sterling can be a considerable factor (of which more later). So treat any index comparisons with caution.

CHOOSING A TRUST: YOUR INVESTMENT AIM

You will know whether you are looking primarily for an income for your investments, or are simply looking for capital growth. If you are seeking income, then you will have to decide how much of your investment should go into fixed interest investments, and how much into equities. If you are seeking capital growth, you will be faced with decisions as to which markets and sectors are likely to prove the most rewarding. In either case, you will have to make a decision about the management group or groups as well.

INCOME

If you are looking for income, the immediate problem to be faced is that investing in equities is not going to provide you with a very high income to start with. The yield on the FT-All Share Index at time of writing is 3.06 per cent; 'High Income' unit trusts might give you a yield of up to 5 or 6 per cent gross, which can only be described as paltry compared with the return you can currently get from a building society.

The point about investing in equities, however, is that they should provide you with a rising income over the years, and some capital appreciation as well. Table 26 shows that, in the past at any rate, going for 'jam tomorrow' rather than today has paid off.

What considerations should you bear in mind when choosing an income unit trust? The basic rule of thumb is that you

Table 26 Equity income trusts: performance compared to building society investment

1. £1,000 invested five years ago	Unit trust*	Building society
a) Income:		
In first year	£67	£99
In fifth year	£96	£86
b) Capital value at end of fifth year	£3,695	£1,000
2. £1,000 invested ten years ago		
a) Income:		
In first year	£57	£61
In tenth year	£124	£86
b) Capital value at end of tenth year	£4,600	£1,000
3. £1,000 invested 15 years ago		
a) Income:		
In first year	£30	£61
In 15th year	£122	£86
b) Capital value at end of 15th year	£4,870	£1,000

*Median equity income unit trust compared to building society higher interest account. Figures as at 1 July 1987
Source: *Unit Trust Association*

should 'go for the lowest yield you can afford'. Mixed income trusts which invest in preference shares as well as equities will provide a higher yield now, but correspondingly less chance of a rising income, or of capital growth.

Even with all-equity trusts, there can be significant differences in the yield level. But the above principle still holds true. The primary aim of the fund managers is to produce a rising income, year by year; an aim which is not always easy to carry out, particularly in the difficult times. The lower the yield, the more choice there is for managers to pick shares which they think have good long term growth prospects.

It is also worth wondering *why* some shares have higher yields than others. The level of yield is, of course, a function of the price of the share. Some shares may have a high yield because the share price has fallen – and it may have fallen for good reason, because the market does not think the company is in good shape. Again, the lower the yield the fund manager has to produce, the more chance there is for him to pick 'blue chip' type stocks, with a middling yield, rather than having to go for the more specialised and possibly more risky high yielding investments.

Past performance is perhaps more relevant in the case of income unit trusts than it is in the more specialist sectors such as gold share trusts, where investment fashions rather than management will largely dictate performance. Looking at the long term dividend record of an income unit trust should give an indication of the manager's ability to produce results. Ideally, income unit trusts should provide an income that rises at least as fast as inflation. This task has proved reasonably easy over the last three years or so, but was much harder to achieve prior to then, when inflation was considerably higher.

What about the capital performance of the trust? You can afford to be more relaxed over this because you are likely to be investing long-term for the income rather than wanting to cash your holding in at short notice. In fact, if you look after the income, choosing a trust with a good and consistent dividend record, then you can more or less leave the capital to look after itself. Good results on the first criterion will almost certainly mean good results as far as the capital is concerned as well. In fact, income unit trusts can provide an unlooked-for bonus on the capital side. This is because there is often a 'recovery' aspect to income trusts. If a share has a higher than average yield, this could be simply because the share has fallen out of favour with the market, and if it recovers, then it will bring above average capital growth for its investors as a extra reward.

If you are choosing an income unit trust for long term investment, there are a number of questions that you need answers to.

1. Does the portfolio consist of all equities, or a mixture of ordinary shares, preference shares and other fixed interest securities?
2. If the latter, what proportion is in ordinary shares?
3. Have dividends increased regularly, in line with, or near to, the inflation rate over a long period?
4. When are distributions made?
5. What is the current yield?
6. Has the capital performance been satisfactory?
7. What is the annual management charge? (Since annual management chanrges are taken out of the income of the trust, this can be important. The lower the charge, the better.)

Not all trusts, of course, have been in existence for long enough to provide past performance statistics. In that case, you can judge only by the type of portfolio (ordinary shares versus the rest), level of yield, and level of charges.

SPECIAL SCHEMES

As mentioned in the last chapter, several groups run monthly income schemes, enabling investors to receive a distribution every month of the year through an investment in a range of that group's income trusts. An alternative is to make up your own 'package' using trusts from different groups, which means you will be able to choose the type of trust yourself, rather than automatically being put into a gilt trust because the group concerned does not have enough equity income trusts available. A third option, run by a couple of groups only is a single trust which pays out income monthly.

Overseas income trusts
A relatively new phenomenon, thanks to recent tax changes, there are now a dozen or so specialist income trusts which invest overseas. The trusts tend to invest in convertibles as well as ordinary shares. They have a higher risk profile than domestic income trusts, as there is the currency factor to take into account. They also tend to have higher annual management charges (1 per cent is typical) which can be a particular disadvantage in an income trust.

A PLEA FOR GENERAL TRUSTS

If you are not investing primarily for income, then it is usually assumed you are investing for growth. But this simple minded division leaves out the stalwarts of the unit trust industry, the *general* trusts, which aim to provide a balanced mix between growth and income.

The basic argument against general trusts is superficially cogent but not valid. Quite simply, general trusts are boring. You will rarely see them at the top of the performance tables, and they simply do not make headlines. They are unlikely to double your money in a year, and even over longer periods such as five years, they will rarely feature in the 'top 10' league.

But they do have considerable attractions. Table 27 shows the performance of the median UK General Fund over various periods, – and if you compare this with the results of the specialist growth trusts shown in Table 28, you will see that what they produce is very far from boring.

Table 27 UK general funds – past performance

Result of £1,000 invested in median UK General fund . . . years ago		
5	10	15
£3,916	£7,513	£8,396

Note: Figures include net income reinvested on an offer to bid basis, as at 1st July 1987.
Source: *Unit Trust Association.*

But as well as good long term performance, general trusts are arguably the least risky of all the sectors, and the least volatile. First-time investors in unit trusts are often attracted by the advertisements for the flashy latest offering from some group – Japanese technology companies, perhaps, or European smaller companies. While an investment case could no doubt be made for each of these, it is sad that general trusts are so easily overlooked, partly, no doubt, because groups themselves do not promote them very actively. But for small or first-time investors, there is a lot to be said for building up a portfolio round the 'core' of a general trust.

GROWTH TRUSTS

Around three quarters of all unit trusts aim purely at producing capital growth for their investors, with income being of practically negligible importance. They encompass UK growth trusts, international trusts, and trusts concentrating on particular overseas markets, indeed, in some cases, particular segments of overseas markets.

Their range makes it difficult to generalise about such trusts and inevitably, impossible to comment about relative investment attractions. The question of which market offers the best prospect at any given time must be answered by the investor or his adviser. However, once you have decided on the broad area you wish to invest in, the following questions should be asked. (Many of the answers will be found in the trust's annual report.)

1 How specialised do you wish your investment to be?
If you want to invest on a very general basis, you can either go for a 'fund of funds' or an international trust; you can also climb one step up the ladder to a single market trust, or two

steps up to a specialist market trust.

Specialisations tend to come and go in the fashion stakes – some names stick, others disappear unlamented (the Motorway Trust was one that fell by the hard shoulder). Names – and the concepts behind them – that have stood the test of time include:

Smaller Companies Trusts – on the principle not only that 'small is beautiful' but that small companies tend to offer more exciting growth prospects than the giants.

Recovery Trusts – companies that fall on hard times can make very rewarding investments if the fund manager picks his shares skilfully.

Special Situations Trust – a mixture of the first two.

Technology Trusts – it is perhaps too early to tell whether 'technology' is going to prove an established sub-sector in unit trusts or will be a relic from fashions of the early 1980s. Technology trusts invest in 'high technology' companies principally in the US and Japan, on the basis that innovation brings rewards. But it has proved one of the most volatile sectors in recent years.

2 Do you wish to invest overseas, or limit your investments to the UK?

Either choice has attendant risks. Staying in the UK means putting all your eggs in a single market; spreading your investment overseas means adding in a 'currency factor' to the 'market risk'.

Once you have decided on the area to invest in, and the degree of specialisation, you must then decide on the particular trust or trusts. There are two ways of reaching a decision:

(a) What is the past performance of the management group? What you should be looking at here is the overall results of a group's management, across all the sectors; and over various periods of time. No groups can be top of all the sectors; but some groups have shown consistently good results, with all or nearly all of their trusts in the upper or second quartile for each sector. The greater the number of trusts a group runs, the harder this will be – but still, some of them manage it. If you are going to switch trusts actively, look for a group with a wide range of trusts that offers a good switching discount.

(b) What is the investment management style? It has never been conclusively proved that one way of managing funds is any better than another – and is not likely to be. However, there

are different styles, and one may suit your attitudes and purposes better than another. Things to ask about are:

Liquidity
Some trusts will go 'liquid' to a considerable extent (50 per cent or more in extreme cases) if the market is falling. Others stay fully invested, believing it is up to the individual to decide whether to be in that market or not.

Concentration
Some trusts run a 'tight ship' investing in no more than 30 stocks – others run portfolios of 200 or more. Specialist growth trusts will tend to have more concentrated portfolios. The fewer the number of stocks, the higher the risk/reward ratio.

Hedging
If you invest overseas, your returns in sterling are affected by the movement of exchange rates as well as the underlying investments. Some fund managers are willing to 'hedge' currency risks (i.e. neutralise the effect of the currency movements) others are very reluctant to do so. It should be pointed out it is something that it is notoriously easy to get wrong.

Management activity
Some trusts are very actively managed, in other words, managers will buy and sell with great frequency; others prefer the 'buy and hold' philosophy. There are obviously many degrees in the middle.

Two other general theories are often advanced as providing valid criteria for choosing a trust: one, that small funds do better and two, that new funds do well. There are probably as many exceptions as the rule in both these cases. As far as new launches are concerned, many of the trusts that have had the wraps taken off in the last year or two have indeed done well. While it is true that the markets have been kind to them, unit trust managers do try hard to get their 'timing' right for new trusts (apart from anything else, it makes their past performance figures look so much nicer if they do!) and a new fund does have the initial advantage over its fellows that it is not, at least, lumbered with past mistakes.

On the 'small versus large' argument, there is again a grain of truth in the theory that small funds are better. They can be more flexible; if they are investing in a specialist area they can buy lines of stock that a large fund would not be interested in. Remember that small is relative and a large US trust (by our standards) is probably miniscule compared to their market.

Finally, there is the old argument on location. Fund managers who are based in London or Edinburgh who are managing overseas trusts will explain with total conviction that their situation is a positive advantage: by being geographically divorced from the area of their investment specialisation they are able to see the wood for the trees, and are less likely to get sucked into the latest fad sweeping the markets. Groups which have offices in the main investment markets in the world, by contrast, point to the benefit of 'on the spot' investment management. There are enough instances and contradictions of each that one is driven to the conclusion that successful fund management depends not so much on where it is carried out, as the degree of intelligence (or luck – or both) that attends it.

ONE FINAL QUESTION FOR YOU

When you are choosing a trust, there is one question of overriding importance that you must ask yourself: are you going to keep a constant watch over your investment or have someone do it for you. If you know, deep down, that you are not really prepared to follow unit prices and market sectors constantly, then you would probably be better off in a less specialist trust. You should in particular avoid those sectors which exhibit strong cyclical performance (commodities and gold share trusts being cases in point).

OFFSHORE FUNDS: THE INVESTMENT CHOICES

For the UK investor, the majority of offshore funds available have no relevance to him. However, because of the restrictions on unit trusts, some offshore funds can prove useful, as they can reach those investment parts other trusts cannot reach.

The two major instances of this are currencies and commodities. Currency funds can be divided into two broad types. Firstly, sterling funds, which aim to benefit their investors either by obtaining wholesale money market rates on short term deposits and/or providing capital gains by locking into longer term fixed interest securities; and secondly, foreign currency funds, which add in the extra excitement of potential gains or losses from exchange rate movements. Foreign currency funds can be of two types. A managed fund, where the managers swop about between different currencies in order to maximise gains, or single currency funds, where the investor picks the currency of his choice (dollars, yen, Swiss francs, etc.)

In all cases, there are two important aspects to take into account: one, the level of charges imposed by the fund (some have initial charges of only 2.5 per cent, others 5 per cent or more) and two, the taxation status of the fund. Funds which distribute at least 85 per cent of their income can apply for distributor status. If granted by the Inland Revenue this means that income will be taxable at the investor's income tax rate, but that any capital gains fall under the more lenient CGT rules.

Funds that 'roll-up' their income are treated differently. Investors are not taxed on the income while it remains in the fund, but as soon as they cash in their investment, they are taxed at income tax rates on *all* the profits they have made, whether they arise from interest or from capital gains made from currency movements. As a rule of thumb, an accumulation fund is best for sterling investments (see Chapter 3). For funds in foreign currencies, especially where a large proportion of the overall returns is expected to arise from capital gains, a fund with distributor status is preferable.

Commodity funds based offshore are a half-way house between the relatively sober commodity unit trusts, which invest in the shares of companies connected with commodities in one way or another, and the thrills and spills of investing in commodities directly, either by investing in 'physicals' (the commodity itself) or in commodity futures contracts (a contract to purchase a fixed quantity of a commodity at a fixed price at a fixed date in the future: the contract can be held until that time or, more commonly, sold on to someone else). Offshore funds can participate in commodities in any of these ways, and are a relatively safe way of doing so, as though you may lose all your investment, you will not be called upon to invest yet more money (which can happen if you are putting money directly into the commodities markets).

To call them 'relatively safe', however, is a bit misleading. They still fall within the category of 'high risk' investments, and no-one, however rich, should have more than 10 per cent of their portfolio in this area, while lesser mortals would probably be better off with nothing at all.

R J THOMPSON & CO.

MEMBERS OF THE STOCK EXCHANGE

Q How do I choose a stockbroker?

A There are several questions you will want answered before making a selection. As a rule of thumb, you will ask in what type of client each firm specialises, when the company was established and what services it offers. You should check whether there is a minimum transaction size and if the firm sets a lower limit on the value of portfolios.

Q Why R J Thompson & Co?

A
- Specialists in private client portfolios
- Personal informed service
- Competitive fees
- In-house research
- Free advice without obligation
- Established, respected firm
- Confidently

Q What service does R J Thompson & Co offer clients?

A We advise on British and overseas shares, units trusts and fixed interest securities. Advice on pensions, assurance and inheritance tax is also available. In addition, one of the firm's partners researches companies as well as producing share circulars at appropriate times. Naturally, we execute transactions quickly and at the best prices obtainable. For expatriate clients, or people who travel overseas for prolonged periods, R J Thompson & Co offers a discretionary and nominee service.

Q Who will I deal with at R J Thompson & Co?

A All private clients deal direct with one of the firm's partners and receive personal attention at a senior level. In contrast, many firms' clients rarely talk to senior managers unless their portfolios are very substantial. At R J Thompson & Co there is no second best.

Q Who do I contact?

A For a confidential discussion of your investment needs, please telephone

Roy Thompson
Sir Charles McLeod Bt

or

Antony Beale
on: 01-588 2790

R J Thompson & Co
1 Salisbury House
London Wall
London
EC2M 5RH

References

We are required under Stock Exchange rules to refer new clients to the Stock Exchange Members' Mutual Reference Society, a registered credit agency for Stock Exchange members dealing with the public.

CHAPTER 8

INVESTMENT TRUSTS

Investment trusts are not trusts, but companies. Their aim in life is to invest their capital somewhere else – in other company shares, in fixed interest securities and the like. Investors who buy investment trust shares are, therefore, getting a 'slice of the action' of a whole portfolio of shares for the price of one. In this respect, they are similar to unit trusts (with which they are often compared and contrasted) and certainly, their basic reason for existing is identical, to provide the small investor with a spread of risk for a modest outlay.

This spread of risk is legally insisted upon by the fact that to qualify for the tax treatment described below, investment trusts cannot invest more than 15 per cent of their assets in any one security, meaning a theoretical minimum portfolio of at least seven. In practice, trusts are likely to have anything between 40 and 200 holdings. The exceptions to this rule are the shares of other investment trust companies, which themselves will automatically provide a spread or risk. They must also distribute at least 85 per cent of the income they receive from their investments to their shareholders.

THE TAXATION POSITION

Investment trusts are similar to unit trusts in that liability to tax on any gains they make belongs to the shareholder, rather than the company itself. This means shareholders can realise up to £6,600 of gains (in the 1987/8 tax year) before being liable to tax.

On the income side, dividends from other companies in which the trust invests are paid net of basic rate tax to the holders of the investment trust shares. Non-taxpayers can reclaim the tax; higher rate taxpayers will have to pay more.

Do investment trusts have a unique selling point? The answer is yes, they have several, some of which may be attractive to investors, others possibly offputting.

THE SHARE PRICE – AND THE DISCOUNT

Share prices move (up or down) basically because of the relative levels of supply and demand for them. This holds as true for an investment trust company as it does for, say, GEC. In this respect, it should be noted, investment trusts are quite unlike unit trusts, where the unit price is calculated strictly according to the value of its underlying investments.

If you carried this operation out with investment trusts, you would almost always find that the value of their holdings came to a higher total than the share price of the trust would indicate. The price of investment trusts shares are, therefore, said to be at a 'discount' to their net asset value.

This discount is a puzzling thing: firstly because it cannot be adequately explained away; and secondly because it is difficult to know whether it is a positive advantage, a positive disadvantage – or neither.

On the first count, there are several reasons why an investment trust company's shares are likely to be at a discount: one is the fact that there are manager's fees to pay (which are not there if you are buying the underlying shares directly); another is the fact that an investment trust's holdings are usually valued at the 'mid-market quotation' – in other words, half way-between bid and offer prices. If the investment trust actually sold its shareholdings, it would get a lower price for them than the 'mid-market' price, so this also helps to explain the discount.

But in many cases, these and other technical factors cannot explain away the size of the discount. Behind it is something much more nebulous – simply, the levels of supply and demand. If investment trust shares are in demand, the discount will narrow; if they are not, it will widen.

Is the discount – which in mid 1987 was standing at an average of around 19 per cent for all investment trusts – a good or bad thing? It depends, it seems, on your point of view. The Association of Investment Trust Companies publish a free booklet, and the title they chose shows at least where they stand: it is called *More For Your Money*. They would argue that a discount has to be a good thing as you are buying a bigger holding in shares indirectly, by investing in the trust, than you would if you have bought them direct. That is fine – except if the discount is still there when you come to sell. If so, you would be getting less money for your investment, in which case the two could cancel each other out!

It is best to think of the discount as a two-edged sword. If stock markets are booming, more people are interested in investing, and the demand for investment trust shares goes up.

So the discount narrows. If markets fall, the discounts tend to widen. Investment trusts can therefore magnify rises in the underlying portfolio – and magnify losses as well. Or in the (adapted) words of the nursery rhyme, when markets are good, investment trusts can be very, very good – but when markets are bad, they are horrid.

One last comment about the discount. There is a limiting factor on how far it can rise. If it gets too large, there are all sorts of hungry predators around – pension funds, for example – who are quite capable of swallowing an investment trust whole. If a trust were standing at a discount of say, 50 per cent, then a pension fund could easily buy up all the shares by offering the shareholders a price based on a discount of perhaps 25 per cent – and still make a healthy profit for itself after all expenses. Another avenue is for the managers to 'unitise' the trust – turn it into a unit trust where units are valued straightforwardly according to the value of the portfolio. Both of these events have happened, more than once, in the investment trust world; and some private investors have bought such shares simply on this premise – that if you can buy them at a large enough discount, something or other along these lines is bound to happen sooner or later, giving you an instant and 'free' profit which bears no relation to the movements in the stock market.

Gearing

The 'magnifying' effect of the discount is itself a form of gearing. But investment trusts can go one better than that: unlike unit trusts, they can borrow money to invest, alongside the shareholders' funds. If, for example, you can borrow money at 10 per cent, and invest it in something that goes up 50 per cent in a year, then you have magnified the profits. (Needless to say, if the stock you are investing in goes *down,* you will have magnified your losses.) An example of how gearing can work in your favour is shown in Table 28. In this case, the borrowing is in the form of a debenture stock.

Charges

Investment trust portfolios are managed full time – and naturally enough, this does not come free. However, there is no initial charge as such; the costs of buying investment trust shares are no different from those for buying other shares. There is an annual management charge that averages about 0.4 per cent of the assets under management (with the discount, it will work out at a slightly higher percentage of the investment trust's share price). Nevertheless, the overall charges compare well with those imposed on unit trusts.

Table 28 Gearing on an investment trust

Capital Structure of trust:
4,000,000 5% debenture stock	£4,000,000
6,000,000 £1 ordinary shares	£6,000,000
	£10,000,000

Assume the portfolio doubles in value over five years and that the debenture stock is repaid at the end of that time. The effect as as follows:

	Year 1	Year 5
Value of portfolio	£10,000,000	£20,000,000
Less debenture stock	£4,000,000	£4,000,000
Assets attributable to 6,000,000 ordinary shares	£6,000,000	£16,000,000
Net asset value per ordinary share	£1	£2.67

Thus, while the portfolio has increased by 100 per cent, the assets attributable to each ordinary share have increased by 167 per cent (from £1 to £2.67).

INVESTMENT CHARACTERISTICS OF INVESTMENT TRUSTS

Investment trusts are not just unit trusts with rather curious knobs (called 'discounts' and 'gearing') on them. They can offer a quite different approach to the business of investment management. There are two basic differences: one, investment trusts are not limited to investing in *quoted* securities, i.e. to companies quoted on the Stock Exchange, the way unit trusts are. They can invest in unquoted securities and in other assets, such as property. This flexibility of investment trusts means they can pursue more exciting (and speculative) investment policies, particularly with specialist 'Smaller Companies' or 'Technology' trusts.

The second difference aids and abets the first. With a unit trust, remember, the managers are obliged to sell or redeem units on demand. The situation with an investment trust is quite different. Shareholders who want to realise their holdings must go to the market and find a willing buyer – those who want to invest must find a willing seller. Either way, it is of no concern to the manager of the trust. He knows exactly how much money he has got to play with, and the movements in the share price do not directly affect him. So he can afford to take much longer term decisions than his unit trust counterpart. Indeed, he can afford to be more speculative, to invest in companies where there is no ready market for the shares, because he knows he will not be forced to realise them if his shareholders want their money back.

Table 29 Investment categories of investment trusts

1	Capital & Income growth: general
2	Capital & Income growth: UK capital growth
3	General
4	International
5	North America
6	Far East
7	Japan
8	Commodities & Energy
9	Technology
10	Income Growth
11	Smaller Companies
12	Special Features

INVESTMENT RANGE

Investment trusts have always had a strong international outlook: In the last century, American Railroad companies were a favourite for the far-sighted (usually Scottish) fund managers. Many still hold substantial North American investments. There are around 200 investment trusts in existence, and a steady stream continue to be launched, though not at the rate at which new units trusts are appearing.

The Association divides trusts into 12 categories (see Table 29) for the purposes of performance comparisons, although investment trusts can be less highly regimented than unit trusts in investment aims – or alternatively, they can be so highly specialised that it is difficult to compare like with like.

Figure 5 shows the average performance of investment trusts over the last four years, to end December 1985, compared to various stock market indices. The strong performance of investment trusts reflects in part a narrowing of the discount over the period.

HOW TO KEEP TRACK OF PRICES

Papers such as the *Daily Telegraph* and *Financial Times* publish share prices of investment trusts daily. On the fourth Saturday of every month, the Association of Investment Trust Companies publishes a listing of trusts, broken down into their various categories, showing a considerable amount of detail including the current share price. The table shows the geographical spread of each trust, the current net asset value, the five year record of the net asset value (*not* the share price, please note – but a good indication nonetheless of the fund managers' achievements). There is also a column for 'gearing'. This shows the percentage amount by which the net asset value would rise if the equity assets held by the trust doubled in value. If the figures are above 100, this means the trust is geared to some extent. This listing is also published in the same papers.

VARIATIONS ON A THEME

Limited life trusts

Whatever the so-called 'advantages' of the discount, some companies have seen it as a drawback, and they have decided to get round it by offering 'limited life' trusts. These either have a fixed redemption date, at which point the company will be wound up and its assets realised at full market value, or a series of dates – perhaps once a year – at which shareholders have the option to vote for the winding up of the company.

Either strategy has the advantage that the discount is unlikely to stray up too far; there can be a drawback, however, in that it means fund managers cannot be as far-sighted in their investment policy as they would with an ordinary investment trust.

Split capital trusts

Split capital trusts are an ingenious idea based on the premise that there are basically two diferent types of investor: the non-taxpayer (whether an individual, charity or pension fund) who is happy with a high income – and the higher rate taxpayer, who is looking for growth but for whom income is pretty much an irrelevance.

Split capital trusts accommodate both types by having two classes of share capital. One that stands in line to pick up all the income from the portfolio of shares (but none of the growth);

the other that benefits from all of the capital growth but none (or in a few cases a very limited amount) of the income. All split capital trusts have a redemption date, and income shares, surprisingly perhaps tend to stand at a *premium* to the fixed price at which they will be redeemed. This makes sense if you think of them as an equity version of a high-coupon gilt which is standing above par.

Capital shares do not have a fixed redemption price; their value will depend on the market value of the constituent shares in the portfolio at redemption date. Their price in the meantime is partly influenced by the level of supply and demand for the shares, and partly by the closeness or otherwise of the redemption date. The nearer this approaches, the more directly will the share price be related to the value of its underlying assets.

One of the advantages of the capital shares for a higher rate taxpayer is that the underlying portfolio of shares do not themselves have to be low yielding – whereas if he was investing directly, he would probably be avoiding anything with a reasonable yield because of its tax inefficiency so far as he was concerned.

SHAW CAVENDISH & Co.

GOLD BULLION COINS

Bought and Sold in Strictest Confidence

For Brochure and details write to:

SHAW CAVENDISH & CO
(Bullion Dealers)

Cavendish House, Chester CH2 2AJ
0244 24315/378595

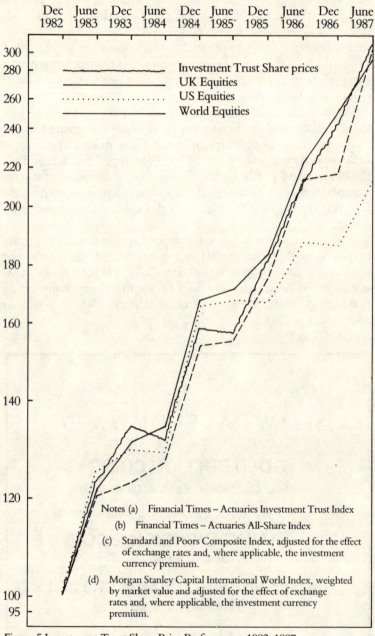

Figure 5 Investment Trust Share Price Performance 1982–1987
Source: *AITC*

Some split capital trusts invest in other investment trusts, so that capital shareholders are in effect getting a 'double discount'. In fact the ramifications do not have to stop there. One such trust invests in other split capital trusts which invest in other investment trusts . . . (one gets the sinking feeling this could go on *ad infinitum,* in fact it does not). Many of the split capital trusts invest directly in equities themselves, while others invest in unit trusts.

Investment trust warrants
These are a fairly recent development; around 40 investment trusts now have warrants attached to them. What you are buying when you buy a warrant is not a share, but a *right to buy* a particular share, at a specified price, on a particular date (or range of dates) in the future.

To take a fictitious example, XYZ Investment Trusts Shares may be standing currently at 220p, and its warrants at 50p. The warrants give you a right to buy shares in XYZ on 1 June 1995 at a price of 200p (called the 'exercise price'). Given that the warrants are costing you 50p now, the price of the shares in XYZ will have to exceed 250p before the transaction becomes profitable – and you have to remember that by buying the warrants rather than the shares now, you are foregoing the rights to any dividends from the shares in the meantime.

But then you have got nearly 10 years in hand, before you need exercise the warrant. Suppose XYZ shares double in that time, and that you have an initial £1,000 to invest. The choice is shown on Table 30.

Table 30 Shares and warrants, the choice

Buying shares		Buying warrants	
Now		Now	
Cost of shares: 220p		Cost of warrants: 50 pence (exercise price: 200 pence, June 1995)	
£1,000 investment buys:			
454 shares		2,000 warrants	
June 1995		June 1995	
Value of shares: 440 pence			
1 Sale proceeds of shares (454 x 440 pence)	£2,000	1 Sale proceeds of shares (2,000 x 440 pence)	£8,800
2 Less original cost	£1,000	2 Less cost of exercising warrant (2000 x 200p)	£4,000
		3 Less original cost	£1,000
			£5,000
3 Profit from transaction	£1,000	4 Profit from transaction	£3,800

This is a simplified example, ignoring costs of buying and selling in each case, while it also ignores the value of the dividends that would have been received by the investor who had bought the shares now, rather than the warrants. Finally, it disregards the fact that the investor who had opted for the warrants could have sold these directly (at any point between now and June 1995) rather than going through the rigmarole of buying up the shares and then selling them again.

WHERE TO FIND OUT MORE

First stop for anyone interested in finding out more about investment trusts is the Association of Investment Trust Companies, Park House, 6th floor, 16 Finsbury Circus, London EC2M 7JJ. As noted, the Association publishes a free booklet, *More for your Money* which gives general background information on investment trusts. The AITC also publish a more comprehensive guide to investment trusts entitled *How to Make It,* a paperback giving details of all trusts available at a cost of £5.95 for the 1987/8 edition (including p & p) from the same address.

For further background reading, there is *Investment Trusts Explained,* by A A Arnaud, published by Woodhead Faulkner, £6.95.

If you are interested in investment trusts, but the amount you have available is so small that it would make the buying and selling prices disproportionately high there are a range of options: several life assurance and pension plans offer funds specialising in the investment trust sector, and there is a range of unit trusts offering a route into the sector. A few investment trust companies also run special schemes themselves for the small investor. The AITC has compiled a listing of all these options.

One word of warning: as this chapter indicates, investment trusts can be complicated animals, and if you are interested in investing in them directly, it is wise to get professional advice. If you are wondering who to go to for this, the AITC also publishes a free booklet called *The Private Investor's Stockbroker List,* which gives details of brokers who are willing and (in their own view, at any rate) able to give advice on investment trusts to private clients.

CHAPTER 9

LIFE ASSURANCE AND FRIENDLY SOCIETY INVESTMENTS

Another large contingent in the cast of thousands who want to manage our money for us are the life assurance companies. Over the last 30 years, life assurance companies have made great strides, away from the rather Victorian, paternalistic approach of offering whole life policies to sensible, modest savers, to a much more investment-orientated attitude, offering a range of sophisticated and highly specialised products. That is not to say their 'traditional' business of term assurance, with-profits endowment policies and the like have gone by the board, far from it. But for the man with a lump sum to invest as opposed to regular premiums, it is by and large the more recent products which are of interest. In this chapter we look at three different offerings from the life assurance companies.

The first are single premium bonds (not those Premium Bonds). These are one more attempt by the professionals in the financial services industry to provide a spread of risk for the small investor alongside unit and investment trusts. Annuities and 'back to back' income plans are vehicles that offer investors a fixed income – and can be considered as an alternative (or additional) to investments such as gilts, National Savings, building societies and Guaranteed Income Bonds.

SINGLE PREMIUM BONDS

Single premium bonds offer investors a wide spread of risk for a small investment – generally £500 or £1,000 as a minimum. They are technically life assurance vehicles, but the amount of 'life assurance' you get is practically negligible – in most cases, it is equal to no more than the original investment. This is because they are devised as investment vehicles: if the insurance element were any higher, it would simply cost extra money and result in higher charges on the bond. As it is, charges on bonds are comparable to those on unit trusts, but the initial charge is sometimes slightly lower.

Like unit trusts, there is a whole range of investment specialisations that bonds can offer – in theory, their range can be even wider, as bonds can invest directly in property as well as fixed interest securities and equities. In practice, many companies do not offer the ultra specialised range of funds that unit trusts do: there is less of the 'Japanese Smaller Company' level of specialisation. On the other hand, bonds offer two investment specialisations untouched by unit trusts. The first are 'Property' funds, investing in a range of commercial property (offices, shops and industrial buildings); the second are 'Managed' funds, investing in a mixture of property, equities and gilts.

Managed funds have always been popular, and will no doubt continue to be. They have the widest spread of risk possible to fit in under one roof, and for the modest and conservative investor they are just about the safest first step into 'asset backed' investments that there is. Table 31 shows the past performance of managed funds over various periods.

Property funds have waxed and waned in popularity, having been viewed as the great white hope of small investors at some times, and a boring backwater at others. One problem property funds have to live with is that their investments are essentially long term (you cannot always sell an office block in a hurry) while their investors may want their money back at short notice. All property funds have a proviso that they may delay repayment of investors' money for up to six months – a rule which is intended to protect the interests of other investors who want to stay in the fund – as forced property sales rarely realise full value. In fact, most funds keep sufficient liquidity to cope with any withdrawals without being forced to realise their investments for cash.

Table 31 Past performance of managed funds

Results of £1,000 invested over the following periods			
	5 years £	3 years £	1 year £
Best	3,073	2,206	1,481
Average	2,300	1,679	1,154
Worst	1,384	1,264	844

Figures to 1 June 1987. On an offer to bid basis.
Source: *Money Management*.

THE TAX POSITION

Since bonds are life assurance vehicles, they come under the particular taxation regime relating to life assurance companies. As far as the fund itself is concerned, income gathered within the fund is taxed at 30 per cent if it is 'franked' income (i.e. dividends from UK equities) and at 35 per cent if it is 'unfranked' income, in other words from fixed interest investments or other sources. CGT is payable on profits realised in the fund, which means a reserve must also be set aside for future tax liabilities on currently unrealised profits.

As far as the bondholder is concerned, a basic rate taxpayer has nothing further to worry about. Higher rate taxpayers do. There is a concession that bondholders may withdraw up to 5 per cent of their original investment every year for 20 years, tax free; this counts as return of capital, and is a cumulative allowance – so investors could withdraw nothing for the first 10 years, for example, followed by 10 per cent for the next 10 (or any similar combination).

The reckoning, however, comes when the bondholder cashes in his investment. At that point, a procedure known as 'top slicing' takes place. The profit from the bond is added up, taking into account any withdrawals that have previously been made, and divided by the number of years a bond has been held. The resulting figure is added to the investor's income for the year in which it is cashed, to determine the rate of income tax applicable. That rate (minus basic rate tax which is already deemed to have been paid) is then applied to the *whole* of the profit.

It sounds a complicated procedure, and so it is, but it has one plain lesson for investors; if possible, they should defer cashing in bonds until such time as they are basic rate taxpayers (perhaps after retirement) at which point, there will be no tax on encashment. A second point to bear in mind is that *partial* withdrawals from a bond (in excess of the 5 per cent allowance) are taxed more heavily than a complete encashment. For this reason, the usual practice is to divide an investment into a number of separate bonds to avoid this: £20,000, for example, would be put into 20 separate bonds of £1,000 each.

INVESTMENT CONSIDERATIONS

Bonds have one plus and one minus point against their name as far as investment is concerned. On the minus side is the fact that CGT is paid on profits made within the bond by the life company. If you were investing in unit trusts instead (for instance) there would be no CGT to pay until you realised your holding – and even then, you would be able to make use of the annual exemption from the tax (currently £6,600 in the 1987/8 tax year).

Some life assurance companies have set up their bonds so that they do not invest directly, but via a unit trust. This roundabout way has an advantage in that it means the fund does not have to pay tax every time the fund manager decides to sell parts of the portfolio; it is 'immunised' until the fund itself has to realise units, perhaps because it is experiencing more withdrawals than income money. This route cannot, however, be used with property funds, as unit trusts are not allowed to invest directly in property.

On the plus side is the fact that you can switch more cheaply between different sectors using the investment bond. This is because the bond is treated as a single investment vehicle which has, inside it, a number of different funds (comprising property, managed, equity, gilt, etc.). Once you are in the overall 'bond' you can switch between the different 'funds' with no tax liability, and at a generally cheap cost compared to switching between unit trusts – it might even be free, though in most cases you will pay either a flat fee of perhaps £25 or a small percentage amount of your investment – perhaps 0.5 per cent.

The nearest equivalent outside life assurance to this are the offshore 'umbrella' funds, described in Chapter 6.

BONDS OR UNIT TRUSTS?

These are two of the most actively promoted investment vehicles, and because of this, it is worth comparing them to see which the best deal for you.

Investment bonds score points if:
you like the idea of a managed fund (or a property fund);
you want to switch between sectors;

you are a high rate taxpayer now, but expect your rate to fall to basic rate at some point in the future, and are attracted by the idea of the 5 per cent tax free 'income' facility in the meantime. you are expecting to use your CGT annual exemption on other assets in your portfolio.

Unit trusts score points for:
greater investment range;
better tax treatment because of the exemption from CGT.

Unless you have a specific reason for choosing a bond, such as those outlined above, you will probably be better off in a unit trust. But it is wise to find some (unbiased!) advice first, if you can.

PERONALISED BONDS

These are single premium bonds designed with the needs of substantial investors who are paying high rates of tax. They enable you to keep your existing portfolio of equities, gilts, etc., invested in a single premium bond of your own. The minimum investment required is usually around £50,000. Personalised bonds have some usefulness for very high rate taxpayers, as they 'shield' investment income from the top rates of tax – but there are drawbacks too and they by no means suit everyone who would be eligible.

BROKER BONDS

Broker bonds are yet another variation on the theme of lump sum investment. They are offered by a number of independent financial advisers, who may be insurance brokers or accountants or general investment advisers. The bond makes use of a life company's investment bond with its range of specialist funds – it is, in fact, a 'bond within a bond'.

How it works is that the adviser will pool all his clients' money into the one bond, and then switch it between the different underlying funds on the basis of changing market conditions. The broker's aim is to achieve a better return for his clients than would be the case if he had just sold them each a bond in the life company's managed fund, for instance, or its international fund.

Some of these bonds have done rather well, more than justifying the 0.5 per cent extra per year that (typically) advisers charge for the service. Others have fared less spectacularly. Therefore there are questions you should ask before investing in such a vehicle.
1 Does your adviser actually know about investment? (There are many people who sell these bonds, insurance brokers, accountants, etc.; ensure that your adviser knows about the stock markets and not just insurance or tax matters.)
2 How has the broker bond performed compared to, say, the average international fund, or international unit trust? (If the results are much the same, why bother to go this roundabout route which costs more?)

ANNUITIES

Annuities provide a fixed income for life at a high level, the drawback being that no capital is returned. There are many variations on the basic concept, which works as follows.
1 The investor hands over a lump sum to a life assurance company.
2 In return, the life company pays him a fixed income for life, at a level which depends partly on interest rates prevailing at the time and partly on the investor's age. The older the investor is, the higher the rates are (because his life expectancy is correspondingly reduced).
3 A proportion of the regular payments are treated for tax purposes as a 'return of the investor's capital' and are therefore not taxable. The rest is taxed at the investor's appropriate income tax rate.

The 'capital element' in the annuity payments is fixed by the Inland Revenue. This also depends on age; the older you are at the time you buy the annuity, the higher the capital element will be as a proportion of the total payment. Some examples of current annuity rates, together with the applicable capital element, are given in Table 32.

ALTERNATIVES TO THE BASIC ANNUITY

The biggest drawback with ordinary annuities is the fact that no capital is returned on death. Even if you were to die the day

Table 32 Annuity rates

Purchase price: £10,000	Gross annuity* (including capital element)	Capital element**
Male aged 65, single life, no guarantee	1,300	705
Male aged 75, single life no guarantee	1,800	1,198
Male aged 65, single life, guaranteed 5 years	1,250	690
Male aged 65, single life, guaranteed 10 years	1,180	641
Male aged 65, female aged 60, joint life last survivor, no guarantee	1,000	425
Male aged 65, female aged 60, joint life last survivor, guaranteed 5 years	1,000	421

* The figures for the gross annuity assume that payments are made half yearly in arrears.
** The capital element is tax-free, counting as partial return of capital. The balance is taxable.
Current rates in July 1987
Source: *7 Day Rate Update*.

after handing over your money, not a penny would be returned to your heirs. Instead you can opt for an annuity which is guaranteed to pay out for a number of years (5, perhaps, or 10). This means payments will continue to be made, for that period of time, even if you died in the meantime. An alternative is a 'Joint Life Last Survivor' annuity. This is designed for couples, and payments continue until the second death. As Table 32 shows, all these variations involve a lower payment to start with.

Another option, designed to tackle the other basic drawback to annuities, that of providing a *fixed* income only, is an increasing annuity, where payments increase by a fixed percentage each year.

The figures in Table 32 for 'Single Life' annuities all relate to the male of the species. Because women live longer, annuity rates for them at any given age are lower (usually equivalent to a man three or so years younger).

Finally, there is one other type of annuity: a 'Temporary

Annuity' which does not pay an income for life, but for a fixed period of time. These are usually only used in conjunction with some other scheme, perhaps to fund a life policy over a 10-year term.

Ordinary annuities can be a useful element in financial planning for elderly people (below the age of around 60, rates are so low they are not worth bothering about) – but only so long as the various drawbacks outlined above are clearly appreciated. They provide better value at times when interest rates are high. It is always worth shopping around if you are thinking of buying one, as rates vary considerably among different life companies. For example, the best rate for a man aged 65 with £10,000 to spend is (at time of writing) £1,399 a year; the worst, £1,202.

'BACK TO BACK' INCOME PLANS

These are packaged schemes offered by various life companies under names such as Income Bonds, Design for Income, Guaranteed Income Plans. Their aim is to provide a fixed income for 10 years, at a level which is reasonably competitive with, say, a building society account, plus some prospect of capital growth. The schemes are a package of two separate elements: a 10 year endowment policy plus a 10 year temporary annuity. The lump sum buys the annuity, and out of the monthly (or sometimes, annual) payments it provides, the regular premium on the endowment policy is paid, leaving a surplus which (after tax is taken into account) is spendable income for the investor. After 10 years of this, the endowment policy matures, which should (hopefully) provide a sum at least equivalent to the initial capital invested.

These schemes can be suitable for a portion of retired people's capital. Because an annuity is involved, they provide better value when interest rates are high. But there are two important points to watch out for.
1 What sort of life cover is provided in the event of the investor dying before the 10 years are up? (Most but not all will provide for a full return of capital.)
2 What sort of investment record has the life company concerned produced on its with-profits endowment policies? (These schemes do not generally require investors to undergo a medical examination.)

Finally, you should always compare them with rates available elsewhere, such as a building society.

FRIENDLY SOCIETIES

The origins of friendly societies (or benefit societies, as they are called in the USA) go back a couple of centuries. They were formed as 'self-help' organisations, often combining social with financial activities, assisting the poor to put money aside. Some have remained largely social, while others have concentrated on financial pursuits and are in many respects similar to life assurance companies, but there are some basic differences. They are not covered by the Policyholders' Protection Act, while they have more strict limits on the type of business they can undertake than life assurance companies.

Friendly societies do, however, have one particularly attractive string to their bow that life companies do not: they can offer *tax exempt* policies, where the investments may grow free of CGT and income tax within the fund, and provide tax-free proceeds to the investor. These policies are 10 year, regular premium contracts. The big drawback of these policies is that the maximum life cover allowed under the contract is £750, which means in turn that the maximum premium allowed is about £9 a month. Many societies that run these policies also offer a 'lump sum' version, where you hand over a sum of money (which varies between about £775 and £1,000, depending on the scheme) in advance, and this is then 'fed' into the plan over the following 10 years.

At least half of the regular premiums must be invested in what are called 'narrow range' securities, meaning fixed interest investments such as gilts, building society deposits, bank deposits and the like. The balance can be invested in 'wider range' securities, meaning equities. Some of the schemes available invest solely in narrow range securities – there are several that have linked up with a single building society, for example – others offer the mixture, with the 'wider range' portion going into a unit trust.

The tax advantages conferred by the scheme vary from contract to contract. As far as a scheme with 50 per cent 'wider range' investments is concerned, if the bulk of the profits on this portion are to come by means of capital growth rather than reinvested income, there is not a great advantage to going this route as opposed to investing your money directly in such wider range securities. Each person, remember, can realise up to £6,600 of capital gains (in the 1987/8 tax year) before paying any tax – and there are also the index-linked provisions which will diminish the 'paper gain'.

The exemption from income tax is, however, of more real benefit to the majority of investors and the schemes that invest totally in 'narrow range' securities (i.e. investments that pay interest but offer no prospect of capital growth) benefit from this exemption to the full.

Friendly society schemes do have limitations, however.
1 Investors are only allowed to take one plan.
2 The amount that can be invested is small.
3 Charges are not always easy to ascertain, and can be high, in proportion to the size of the premiums.
4 If the plan is surrendered before the end of 10 years, returns are limited by law to the total amount of premiums paid.
5 The investment policy is restricted by the requirement that 50 per cent of premiums must go into narrow securities.

For all that, the tax-favoured status can outweigh all these drawbacks, and friendly society schemes can provide a useful home for the relatively small amount of capital they are allowed to accept.

CHAPTER 10

PENSION PLANNING

Pensions are a highly tax favoured form of investment, but very inflexible. The tax concessions are there to encourage people to save for their old age – and logically enough, perhaps, the bulk of the proceeds from a pension plan must be taken in the form of an income, rather than cash.

Pensions are beginning to be a subject of great debate. From April 1988, employees will have the right to take our a personal pension instead of being a member of their company pension scheme. They will be addition be able to opt out of SERPS – the State Earnings Related Pension Scheme.

This new freedom imposes some really quite difficult choices on individuals. It is worth emphasising the difficulty of this decision which arises in part because of the very different natures of the 'final salary' type of company pension scheme, and the 'money purchase' type of personal pension plan.

In a 'final salary' type scheme, a member retires on a pension which is related to the level of his final salary at retirement, whatever that may be. The maximum under Inland Revenue rules is two-thirds of final salary and a typical company scheme provides $1/60$th of final salary for every year a member has been employed. If you've worked there 40 years, therefore, you have reached the two-thirds level.

The important feature of this type of scheme is that it is the company that carries the can. Suppose that in the last 10 years of your working life inflation has roared away, so you end up on double the salary you'd been expecting just 10 years previously. That means your pension will also be double.

Of course, the investments in the scheme may also have done well. But if there is any shortfall at the time you retire, that's not your problem; the company simply has to cough up the extra. And suppose, to make matters worse, the investments have not done well, and markets are going through a terrible bear phase at the time you retire. Once again, it's not your problem; the company has taken on the responsibility and you will get the exact fraction of your salary as pension that your length of service entitles you to, come what may.

There's little doubt that if you're in a good final salary scheme – one that is based on sixtieths of salary, provides the legal maximum of four times salary on death before retirement, and gives periodic increases to its pensioners after retirement – *and* if you expect to stay within that company until retirement, then you should sit tight and ignore all the hullabaloo about personal pensions.

With personal pensions, you see, that risk and that responsibility is all-yours. If inflation gallops, if stock markets crash, making mincemeat of all your plans, it's up to you alone to do something about it.

So why should anyone contemplate a move next year? There are three reasons. One, not all final salary schemes are good. Two, there are government incentives in the shape of rebates from National Insurance Contributions. Three, perhaps most importantly, the final salary type scheme is not so good for the person who leaves before retirement. Anyone leaving such a scheme now will have most of his pension benefits 'frozen'. To take an example, if you've worked for that company for 10 years, seven years' worth of your pension entitlement or thereabouts will be frozen if you leave tomorrow; in other words, your old company will pay you a pension when you finally retire of $7/60$ths of your salary – *at the level it was when you left the company*.

And once again, if inflation (and subsequent promotion) makes that figure look absurdly small, it's tough luck on you, that's all you'll get. From January 1985, any 'preserved rights' accrued under final salary type schemes have to be re-valued once a year. But there is an upper limit here of 5% or inflation, whichever is the less – and this obligation is not backdated tc any previous years. So although this portion of your pension will be slightly higher, the pension prospects overall are not that wonderful.

With a personal pension, on the other hand, you don't lose out by changing jobs at all. All the money that's been invested in your particular pension pot can move with you and just carry on growing.

That is merely a thumbnail sketch of the decisions people may have to face. To make things more complicated: some company schemes are not 'final salary' type at all, but money purchase. A money purchase scheme works essentially like a personal pension. There's a pension pot, into which both company and employee contribute, and the size of the pension you get on retirement depends on how well the pot has grown. If you leave the company before retirement, that 'pot' is portable, so you don't have the problem of frozen pensions.

And then to make matters even worse, there is the distinction between schemes that are 'contracted out' and those that are 'contracted in'. This refers to whether the scheme is part of SERPS, the state pension scheme that is payable in addition to the basic old age pension. At present, the only schemes that can be 'contracted out' are final salary type schemes, and they have to guarantee that the benefits they provide will be at least as good as SERPS. But from next April, company money purchase type schemes and 'appropriate' personal pension schemes will also be allowed to contract out. That means bigger national insurance rebates and more risk.

So people will have, in effect, two decisions to make: one, do they leave their present scheme next April? and two, if they do, should they also 'contract out' of SERPS?

There seems to be a consensus emerging that if you're over 45 or thereabouts you should stay in SERPS. If you're younger, it's worth getting out and using the National Insurance rebates to fund your own personal pension plan. There is also broad agreement that if you are expecting an active career pattern, changing jobs frequently, you're probably better off with a personal pension or, if your company provides one, a money purchase type company scheme.

There are always exceptions and I wish I could say with confidence that there will be expert independent financial advice available to those who are puzzled. Unfortunately, intermediaries will be rewarded only by selling personal pensions rather than advising people to stay where they are, and this may colour their advice – at least that of the less responsible ones.

But in any case, it will finally be up to you to make the decision. No one can tell you what will be *the* best thing to as it depends on so many imponderables.

Meanwhile, there is another change about to happen on the pensions scene – and (in theory) somewhat faster. From October 1987, employees will be allowed to join a 'free standing' AVC scheme instead of the company AVC scheme. AVC stands for Additional Voluntary Contribution and an AVC scheme is a means by which an employee who has joined a company pension scheme late in his working life (and so will clock up less than 40 years' service with the company) can increase his pension towards the maximum two-thirds of income.

For some people in good final salary schemes, this will be a better alternative than any other.

What does all this have to do with lump sum investment? You can look at it two ways. One, providing a proper income for yourself after retirement has to be one of the first aims of any investment plan – who wants to live on the £39-odd a week that the basic old age pension provides? And two, pensions are enormously tax efficient so if you can direct your investments through this route, so much the better.

Pension premiums qualify in full for relief at your highest marginal rate of tax – ie, up to 60% – while pension funds attract neither income nor capital gains tax. In addition, when you retire, you can take a cash lump sum of up to £150,000 out of your pension plan – once again, tax-free. (You can only take it if it's there, of course, and there are various Inland Revenue rules to ensure that the major part of your pension fund is taken as income over the years, not cash.)

A good rule of thumb for any investor – at least, anyone past 40, say – who comes into an extra windfall of some sort, is to think 'pension' first:

* If he's an employee in a company pension scheme (and doesn't want to leave) he could put an extra sum into an AVC scheme;
* If he's an employee with no company pension scheme arrangement, he could put it into a personal pension plan;
* If he's self-employed, he could put it into a personal pension plan.

Of course, some people might have such perfect pension arrangements that there's no need for them to do so. And you should bear in mind that there are regulations both as to the maximum amount you can put in (briefly, 17½% of your annual salary each year into a personal pension; a total of 15% (including AVCs) into a company pension) and the maximum you can take out. If you 'overfund' for your pension you can be quite harshly penalised, so look before you leap.

But as a matter of fact, many people are nowhere near these limits – and as personal pensions catch on, and it is no longer obligatory to save large sums for a pension, I think this problem will increase. I have yet to meet anyone who thoroughly enjoys putting money aside for a pension and going by my own experience as a self-employed individual for four years, it was a constant battle to persuade myself to put real money away in a pension.

Table 33 was a great help in winning the battle and I suggest anyone starting a money purchase type of pension plan (whether it is a personal pension, or joining a company's money purchase scheme) should contemplate these figures from time to time.

Table 33 How much should you put into a pension plan?

The columns show what level of pension (expressed as a percentage of final salary) can be expected, assuming that contributions of 10 per cent of salary are made each year.

Age now	Pension at age 65	
	Male %	Female %
30	58.9	53.4
35	47.6	43.2
40	39.5	35.8
45	28.7	26.0
50	20.6	18.7
55	14.7	13.3

These figures assume a 2 per cent 'real' growth rate on the pension fund, and that pension contributions keep pace with salary increases, i.e. they are always 10 per cent of salary. They also assume that all the fund is taken as a pension, rather than a proportion as a lump sum.
The figures for women are lower at all ages because pension rates are lower for women (they live longer).

Source: *Allied Dunbar*.

WHERE TO FIND OUT MORE

All of us will be hearing a lot more about personal pensions in the coming months. If you're contemplating taking one out, I recommend you read *'Your New Pensions Choice: An Explanatory Guide'* by John Wilson and Bryn Davies. Published by Tolley's at £2.95, it is definitely worth working your way through. *The Daily Telegraph Pensions Guide* is now also available, published by Telegraph Publications at £10·45.

For those in company pension schemes, The Occupational Pensions Advisory Service (OPAS) is a charitable body which can advise members of company pension schemes on their rights. OPAS can be contacted via Citizens' Advice Bureaux or at OPAS, Room 327, Aviation House, 129 Kingsway, London WC2.

More retirement income

If you are retired, or planning for retirement, you need the best possible income from the capital you have, and probably help in reducing the amount of tax you pay. At Imperial Trident we specialise in investment schemes which are particularly advantageous for the over 50's and 60's.

So if you need more retirement income simply phone or send the FREEPOST coupon today.

We're confident we can help.

IMPERIAL TRIDENT

To: Imperial Trident Life Ltd., FREEPOST, London Road, Gloucester GL1 3BR. Tel: Gloucester (0452) 500500.   MRI/GLI/9:87

I should like to obtain more retirement income (minimum capital £1000).

Name_____

Address_____

_____

Postcode_____
(Not applicable in Eire).   A member of the Laurentian Group.

CHAPTER 11

TANGIBLES AND OTHER INVESTMENTS

Tangibles are often dubbed 'alternative investments' which indicates their essential difference to all other investments described so far. Everything else, whether it is a building society account or the most speculative growth stock, is valued ultimately by the income it produces, or might produce some time in the future (possibly even decades ahead). But tangible investments, by their very nature, cannot produce an income. The returns they provide for their investors depend ultimately and solely on the prices other buyers are willing to pay for them, and the factor of rarity (incomprehensible if you tried to apply it to a building society account!) plays a major part.

Tangible investments vary enormously. Pop records from the 1960s, oil paintings by the old masters, Dinky toys and gold bars are all unceremoniously lumped together as tangible investments, but they should not be. Instead, they can be divided into five loose groupings.

Intrinsic
Objects whose value is solely or largely intrinsic, for example, gold or platinum bars, other precious or rare metals, loose diamonds. There is little or no artistic or cultural pleasure to be derived from owning these – indeed, their buyers will often willingly forego the pleasures of ownership by storing the stuff in a bank vault. Their value is one of quality and rarity.

Artistic
Oil paintings, antique furniture, watercolours, statues, 'museum objects' of great value which are undeniably, inevitably 'art', however much their current owners might view them solely as an 'investment'. The prices these 'investments' fetch are outside the reach of the majority of us (who probably could not afford the insurance premiums and alarm systems, let alone the prices themselves).

Collectable
Risking the wrath of all stamp, coin, and old bond certificate

lovers, these are put in a separate category because they do not live up to my definition of 'art'. The investment charcteristics of this sort of tangible are firstly, that collections (in the true sense of the word, showing discrimination and judgement rather than a random accumulation) can often have more value as a whole than in their constituent parts, and secondly, partly following on from that, the most successful investors for this type are those who know and love their subject, the true enthusiasts. The irony is the best investors are those who do not see themselves as 'investors' at all, but collectors.

Ephemeral
Things like biscuit tins, recent first editions and old coronation mugs all fall under the banner of 'ephemera'. Unless you have an extremely large attic, you will find it difficult to embark on a serious course of investing in the ephemera of the future. Typically, only items in the best conditions are valuable and the major reason they have any value is because they are the sort of object most people kick about, rough up, break or throw away.

'Collectibles' (in quotes) are a very different matter. These are the specially boxed sets of coins, or stamps, or 'collectors' items' of china plates, clocks and so on. Items where the advertising usually contains the line 'for you and your family to treasure'. These can miss the investment boat altogether: they do not qualify for our category of 'collectible' noted above, basically because they cheat – they are an adman's (or manufacturer's) idea of a 'collection' but not the real thing. They do not qualify for this category either simply because most people who buy them will keep them carefully, thus failing the 'rarity' test. Of course, they may eventually become valuable, say in a hundred years or so, by which time the majority will have been lost or discarded or sat on – but most of us are hoping for rewards over a rather shorter term than that.

Usable
Into this category go the nicest things: Victorian jewellery, Georgian silver, hand-carved chess sets, fine rugs, signed prints. Objects that can be used and do not lose too much of their value in the using, objects that can be admired for their workmanship, the beauty of their materials, or both. Perhaps

these are the least 'investment-orientated' tangible but (as a personal view) the most happy choice, for those of us who are not speculators (try gold futures) or millionaires (oil paintings) or capable of the single-minded enthusiasm that distinguishes the true collector.

The following pages deal very briefly with some of the major tangible investment opportunities open to investors. When considering any of these as an investment, it should be borne in mind that there are five major points to take into account.
(a) They pay no income – on the contrary, will often cost you money to insure and/or store;
(b) the margin between buying and selling is often much higher than is the case with conventional investments, and as such should be viewed as especially long term;
(c) in many cases, investors will need, and must rely on, the advice of an expert in the field, which can place them in a very vulnerable position;
(d) tangible investments in general have been most popular and produced the highest real returns at times of exceptionally high inflation, when confidence in money and monetary investments has been lost; and lastly,
(e) they are most suited to individuals who are higher rate taxpayers (to whom the loss of income is of less importance) but should never, as a rule, comprise of more than 10 per cent of anyone's total investment portfolio.

GOLD

The simplest and cheapest way to invest directly in gold is to buy a gold coin: a one ounce Krugerrand, a British Sovereign or Canadian Maple Leaf, for example, all of which carry relatively low premiums over the basic gold price. Avoid the half ounce or smaller coins – the smaller the coin, the higher the premium.

Coins bought in this country attract VAT at 15 per cent; it is more sensible to buy 'offshore' in the Channel Islands, for example, and store them there in a bank. Your bank can arrange the purchase of gold coins, either here or in the Channel Islands. They will also buy them back from you.

Given the recent troubles in South Africa, Maple Leafs are probably the most acceptable gold coin (carrying a lower premium than Sovereigns). They can be bought from companies such as Spinks & Son and the Gold Coin Exchange.

Gold has not been a good investment in the last few years, though sterling investors have enjoyed some profits thanks to the decline in the pound against the US dollar (the currency in which gold is traditionally priced).

Indirect investment exposure to gold can be gained by investing in gold shares. They can be bought directly, or via a managed fund such as a unit trust or an offshore fund, the latter may also invest in gold itself and in gold futures. Shares of gold mining companies tend to anticipate movements in the gold price rather than reflect it. They also tend to be more volatile and can be highly geared (shares of mines that are marginally profitable at current gold prices will rise disproportionately to an increase in the gold price). Buying gold futures or taking out bets on the price of gold are the most highly geared means of investing and consequently can prove a rapid way of losing money.

PLATINUM

Investors can buy bars of platinum or coins. The Isle of Man Noble is a one ounce platinum coin: similar considerations to buying gold coins apply here. Platinum is fifty times rarer than gold, but does not occupy the same central position as a store of value that gold does. Its supporters point to the increasing industrial demand for platinum as a good omen for long-term investment.

DIAMONDS

The value of diamonds depends on 'the four Cs': colour, clarity, cut and carat (weight) but to a layman, only the last of the four is readily ascertainable, assuming he has access to sufficiently accurate scales.

Diamonds were wonderful investments in the 1970s and have been pretty awful investments in the 1980s. Conventional thinking dictates that only the 'best' diamonds in terms of colour, cut and clarity, weighing a minimum of one carat, are suitable for investment purposes; but these were the stones whose value was chased up by investor demand to unrealistic heights in the late 1970s. An alternative approach to buying a single high quality stone would be to go for a collection of stones of lesser quality and smaller weights, giving a more 'liquid' portfolio (as you would be able to realise parts of your collection rather than having to sell the entire investment in one go).

In either case, you will be completely in the hands of the experts. Diamonds bought for investment purposes are generally 'loose' i.e. unset. Buying jewellery is usually thought of as a poor second: you are paying too much for the workmanship, so there is less 'intrinsic' value. In addition, jewellery bought through retail shops involves wide margins, typically up to 100 per cent.

The purchase of other precious stones (emeralds, sapphires, rubies) follows these general rules with one further dictat in the case of emeralds. Emeralds are very fragile (excess heat, cold or a hard knock can produce cracks in the stone) and consequently can reduce rapidly in value; careful storage would need to be considered.

WINE

Investing in wine can be risky, particularly if you get caught at the wrong end of some passing fashion. If you get the fashion element right, however, you will enjoy good rewards. In the middle are the acknowledged 'good' wines, mainly bordeaux, possibly burgundy, and vintage ports, all of which take some years to mature. There is less risk here, but rewards are correspondingly less, being essentially linked to interest rates; someone has to hold the wines until they are drinkable and whether it is an individual or a wine merchant, they will expect an appropriate reward for tying up their capital. There may still be a long term growth prospect given the increasing amount of wine being drunk, and increasing interest in fine wines.

If you are considering an investment, remember that proper storage conditions are essential. Minimum investment: around £500 to £2,000.

There are numerous books on wine, for example, Hugh Johnson's *Wine Companion,* published by Mitchell Beazley. Christie's and Sotheby's both hold regular wine auctions.

CARPETS

Persian rugs and antique Chinese carpets may prove a good investment, if they are bought from a reputable dealer. Buying from a shop usually involves paying a high mark-up; buying through an auction can mean acquiring substandard goods at inflated prices. Minimum investment: £200 to £3,000.

For further reading, try *Rugs to Riches: An Insider's Guide to Oriental Rugs* by Caroline Bosly, published by Allen & Unwin.

FORESTRY

Investment in forestry can make sense for wealthy individuals because of the considerable tax concessions and government grants available. Forestry can be a way of building up a long-term investment for the following generation, or rather – given its extreme long term nature – the generation beyond that. The traditional route is to buy the bare land and plant it (making use of Government grants available), opting to be taxed under Schedule D, which means that all costs are offset against the investor's other income. The investment is then passed on to a younger generation (making use of the 50 per cent reduction in value for inheritance tax purposes as it qualifies as a 'business asset').

Income generated from woodlands first begins around 25 years after planting. At this stage it is preferable that the woods are taxed under Schedule B, which means there must have been a change of ownership, as election for Schedule D is irrevocable for the owner. Most timber reaches its full maturity around 75 years after planting.

A minimum direct investment is likely to be of the order of £40,000, although it is also possible to buy part shares for rather less from a forestry management company. Over the (very) long term, the outlook for timber prices is good, given the increasing demand. However, if you are looking for short-term or medium-term rewards, this is not the place for you.

THEATRE PRODUCTIONS

Perhaps the most glamorous of alternative investments. If you have between £500 and perhaps £3,000 to spare, you may like to become an 'angel' – someone who puts up capital for West End theatre productions.

Angels must develop a saintly attitude to losing money: it is estimated that around 90 per cent of shows are not successful enough to return their investors' original capital. But there are the legendary successes (*Cats, Evita*) to spur you on. Remember that the production must recoup enough in ticket sales not just to cover initial expenses (which can be anywhere between £40,000 and £800,000) but running costs as well. The two major pieces of advice given are firstly, remember that critical acclaim is not the same thing as commercial success; and secondly, that the best approach is to back a successful producer rather than choosing the particular production yourself.

The Society of West End Theatre Managers can provide further information, and put you in touch with producers.

The Society of West End Theatre Managers
Bedford Chambers
Covent Garden
London WC2
01-837 0971

BUSINESS EXPANSION SCHEME

The Business Expansion Scheme (BES) was first introduced in the 1983 budget. The aim is to encourage individuals to invest in small unquoted (possibly new) companies by granting full tax relief on the investment. A maximum of £40,000 may be invested in each tax year. In the 1986 budget, the scheme was given an 'indefinite' life – previously it had been due to end in April 1987. 'Indefinite' may, of course, mean until the next General Election.

Investment can be made directly into a qualifying company or via a pooled BES fund. Investing via a fund (which usually involves a minimum commitment of £2,000 plus) is less risky in that money will be spread across a number of different companies, which will have been vetted by the fund's managers. Against this, however, is the fact that management charges may be high and the managers may be under considerable pressure to find the right opportunities quickly: tax relief may only be claimed in the tax year in which the shares are issued. This means that by the end of March in any year, BES funds must be fully invested, otherwise members will lose out on tax relief for that year.

Investors must keep their shares for a five-year period before selling, otherwise there will be a proportionate 'clawback' of tax relief. Since the companies must initially be unquoted to qualify, it is necessary to find out what arrangements are envisaged at the end of the five years. Unless the company goes on to the Stock Exchange, the USM or the Third tier market at the end of that time, investors may have difficulty in realising their investments. A tax concession introduced in the 1986 budget now allows the first disposal of BES shares after the qualifying five-year period to be exempt from CGT.

Some businesses have been specifically excluded from the scheme – basically those that involve little or no risk, for example, businesses concerned primarily with property, farmland or financial services or those which are heavily 'asset-backed', for example, a restaurant or nursing home – where there is little risk involved in the investment.

Investing in BES is unavoidably high risk, even if the fund route is chosen, though they can produce high rewards. Because of the tax incentives, they can make most sense for the high rate taxpayer as he will at least enjoy the certain benefit of substantial tax relief, thus cutting down considerably on the total risk taken.

Professional advice should be sought before investing in this scheme. Some of those that have appeared recently have involved considerable fees for the promoters and other experts involved in the scheme, but with rather less going into the business itself. Many stockbrokers now run a BES 'vetting' service. There is also a specialist magazine on the subject – *The BES Magazine,* available from Private Investor Publications, 1-3 Berry Street, London EC1V 0AA (published monthly).

BECOMING A MEMBER OF LLOYD'S

Wealthy individuals who are prepared to accept the prospect of unlimited liability can apply to become members of Lloyd's, the insurance market. Full membership is restricted to those who have at least £100,000 in readily realisable assets (excluding their house) although it is also possible to join together with other members ('Names') with a smaller amount.

To join, an applicant must be supported by two existing members of Lloyd's and must satisfy the committee that he or she is a 'proper person' to do so, as well as passing the means test. There are currently around 21,000 Names and a long waiting list. If an applicant is accepted, he will join one of the 400 syndicates doing business at Lloyd's. He should make enquiries about the syndicate he hopes to join before election: the last seven years' 'closed' accounts are made available for this purpose.

Underwriting profits or losses in any year are not finally assessed until three years have passed, and new members will therefore see no profits until that time. It should be stressed, however, that members are liable, in the event of losses, without limit – *all* their assets including house and furniture can be called upon in the event of an underwriting disaster.

Membership of Lloyd's has generally been a profitable experience, but there have been some recent and well-publicised cases of losses, while the previously excellent reputation of Lloyd's has also been tarnished as various scandals have come to light.

The taxation of profits from underwriting is a complicated matter and individuals would be well advised to discuss the implications with their accountant before going ahead.

For more information, contact:

Lloyd's of London
Lime Street
London EC3M 7HA
01-623 7100

PENSIONS

We offer independent expert advice on:-
COMPANY SCHEMES – UK AND EX-PATRIATE
SELF-EMPLOYED PENSIONS
ADDITIONAL VOLUNTARY CONTRIBUTIONS
LOCKED-IN PENSION BENEFITS
OPEN MARKET OPTIONS
PENSION LOANS AND FRINGE BENEFITS

Ring **BRIAN MOORE** LL.B., F.C.I.I. NOW
on **0483 810334**

or write in confidence to:-

Eurotax Consultants Limited

Freepost, 3 Lloyds Avenue, London EC3B 3LE.
D.T.Gd

CHAPTER 12

WHERE TO GO FOR PROFESSIONAL ADVICE

One of the most common questions asked by investors is also one of the most difficult to answer: where can I get proper financial advice? The difficulty does not lie in the lack of choice, but the opposite. There are certainly thousands and possibly tens of thousands of different firms and organisations offering advice of one sort or another, with varying degrees of competence, scope, costs and independence.

The first distinction to be made is between the types of advice proffered. Many services concentrate on 'asset management': in other words, you provide the capital sum, they will decide where to invest it for you. But there is another side to financial planning: the side that concerns tax planning, pensions, life assurance. Some firms cover both aspects; some concentrate on one or the other.

The traditional sources of advice were merchant banks, stockbrokers, clearing banks and accountants, and these generally speaking aimed at the 'top end' of the market, while insurance brokers and life assurance agents covered the bottom end of the market. In the last decade or so, these two extremes have in many ways been moving closer together: stockbrokers (particularly in the last year or two) have been valiantly trying to become more accessible to the man in the street (i.e. those without a 'family broker') while small firms of insurance brokers and other financial advisers have been steadily increasing their range upwards, so that they advise, not just on shilling-a-week life policies, but, for example, on tax planning schemes involving substantial sums of money.

The main impetus for these changes, most people are agreed, is the private property phenomenon. The growth in home ownership between the wars has meant that 'ordinary' people are now inheriting the proceeds of the family home: a capital sum of perhaps £50,000, which calls for more than just a choice of building society. To this can be added firstly, the (rather less welcome) increase in taxation, so that it affects far more people more heavily than before, and secondly, (again, not so pleasant) the number of redundancies, bringing lump sum redundancy payments in their wake.

To compound these long-term social changes are the rapid changes now taking place in the financial services industry. The Financial Services Act, which is due to become fully effective some time in 1988, lays down a radically restructured framework for the industry. We went into some detail on this in Chapter 5; but the Act has also introduced a new concept which is extremely relevant to the topic of financial advice: the concept of *polarisation*.

Once the Act becomes fully effective, financial advisers will have to be *either* completely independent of any product company, or exclusively tied to one single company. Until now, a lot of advisers have been, in practice if not in name, only semi-independent. The bank manager, for example, would probably lean towards advising his customers to buy his bank's unit trusts, assuming they have a suitable range, while using other companies' products to a limited extent. Many financial advisory firms would be largely tied into one life company, but perhaps use three or four others for particular products.

The Securities and Investments Board (SIB), the body which has been set up to oversee the implementation of the Financial Services Act, decided this was too confusing for the customer, who might be misled into thinking he was getting fully independent advice, when in reality he was effectively getting one company's sales spiel. So they devised this principle of polarisation.

This, it has to be said, has had some rather odd consequences. The banks in particular have been faced with a difficult choice and at the time of writing at least two major ones have not decided which way to jump. They don't want to reduce the traditional role of the bank manager to merely that of a salesman for his company's products; on the other hand, bank branches have been very useful sources of business for the banks' unit trust and life companies. If the bank branches were to 'polarise' on the fully independent side, there would be no guarantee that the business would continue flowing in.

An independent financial adviser will have to follow two cardinal rules under the new regime, which have been summarised as:

'Know your customer' and
'give best advice'

Expanded a little, what they mean is that an adviser must get to know all the relevant facts about his client – age, tax position, investment and income needs, attitudes to risk and so on – before advising him what to do. And having gleaned all these relevant facts, and decided on the broad advice to give, he must then choose the best products out of all these available, bearing in mind such matters as charges, past investment performance and so on for his client.

The first rule is really common sense, and the second is what any financial adviser worth his salt should be doing anyway. But it is quite a new departure for these rules to become enshrined in law.

As far as company representatives are concerned, incidentally, they too must follow these rules, though in watered-down fashion; as they are tied to just one company's products, their recommendation must simply be for the most appropriate within that company's range.

Coming back to the banks, those that have made the decision have opted for their branches to have 'tied' status, meaning that the only advice you will receive from a branch will concern the bank's own products. However, the banks concerned also have separate advisory companies which will be fully independent.

Building societies, too, are facing this decision as they too give financial advice – at present, it is largely limited to advising on endowment policies for mortgages, but they are keen to get more deeoply involved. At the time of writing, some have decided to go fully independent, others to become tied agents of one company.

The good intentions behind polarisation (to prevent the customer being misled) will, it seems, work only if customers make sure they know on which side of the great divide their adviser stands.

So it is not surprising that the financial advisory industry is in a state of flux as it gears itself up to cope with this quite changed state of affairs. At least it means there is plenty of choice for consumers, though it also means that the business of choosing between them is much harder. What follows is not much more than thumbnail sketches of the main types of adviser and the services they offer at the present time.

THE MERCHANT BANKS

Merchant banks have always been at the top end of the

hierarchy. Many require a minimum portfolio of £250,000 before they will manage it for you (at least one requires a million pounds' worth of free assets). The service they offer is generally discretionary, meaning they have the discretion to make changes in your portfolio, informing you of them after the event. The service will provide management of UK equities and gilts, the management of any overseas holdings, although (even at this level) overseas investments may be made by means of unit trusts and other pooled funds.

Their service will typically provide regular performance reports and valuations, and will cope with all the paperwork involved in an actively managed share portfolio. For this, you can expect to pay a fee of perhaps 0.75 per cent of the value of the assets under management each year. Although the service is discretionary, you will obviously have a say in the main aim of your portfolio. Is it to produce capital growth or income? Do you want a strong emphasis on safety or are you prepared to invest in some high risk investment as well?

THE STOCKBROKER

Stockbrokers have been shinning down their ivory tower in the last few years, as their traditional client base (which could be described as the upper middle class and above) has been fading away, due to tax, death duties – and old age. A number of firms are launching new packaged services, hoping to attract the new wave of people with money to invest.

A few years ago, the only way to find a stockbroker was to write to the Stock Exchange in London, and they would provide you simply with a list of names and addresses of brokers willing to take on new business. Now the firms themselves are advertising and producing booklets on their new services, and it is possible to get a much clearer idea of what they offer than before.

These days, it is quite common for them to offer a range of services as listed below:
1 A 'no frills' dealing service, where you make all the decisions, and simply instruct your broker to carry out your wishes.
2 An asset management service for the smaller investor (with a minimum portfolio requirement of perhaps £5,000 to

£10,000) where equity investments will be held by means of unit trusts or offshore funds, plus direct gilt holdings. There may be no fee as such for this service, as the broker gets commission.
3 An asset management service for the larger investor, which may include management of direct holdings in UK equities. These generally require a minimum portfolio of £25,000 to £50,000.
4 A financial planning service, which will cover advice on pensions, inheritance tax, life assurance, school fees planning – all the other bits, in other words, of financial planning that are not covered by 'investment'.

The one service that has rather disappeared under the wave of these new packages is the traditional role of the traditional stockbroker, whom you could ring up for a general chat about the state of the world and the state of the markets whenever you felt like it, and who was far too gentlemanly to suggest that you should have at least £50,000 before he would apeak to you. In fact, it is premature to announce the death of the traditional stockbroker; he is alive and well, but he is mainly living in the provinces, and working for a small or middle-sized firm.

On the asset management services, some brokers will offer investors a choice between discretionary and non-discretionary services; others insist on being given discretion, as it is much more convenient (and probably cheaper) for them to operate in this way. They tend not to charge a fee for their services, being rewarded out of commissions made on buying and selling; however, this may change in the future.

ACCOUNTANTS

Accountants have traditionally hogged the tax side of financial planning, but it is increasingly recognised that the division between tax planning and investment is a leaky one, two sides of the same coin. Some firms have started to offer overall 'financial planning' services, including investment advice on unit trust holdings. Accountants tend to charge a fee for their services, based on the amount of time spent on your affairs and usually they offset against this any commissions they receive – but again, do ask.

MEMBERS OF FIMBRA

FIMBRA – the Financial Intermediaries, Managers and Brokers Association – is due to become one of the Self Regulatory Organisations (SROs) which, under SIB, are responsible for seeing that the provisions of the Financial Services Act are followed. The majority of independent financial advisers will belong to FIMBRA before the year is out, for the simple reason that it will become a criminal act to carry on an investment business if not properly authorised by the appropriate SRO. I do apologise for this pléthora of initials, incidentally – I don't know how to avoid them.

Members will be subjected to a vetting procedure on joining, must obey certain rules such as always keeping clients' money in a separate bank account, and will be subject to spot checks by FIMBRA officers to ensure that they are carrying on the business properly.

This is perhaps the most difficult category to make generalisations about. Some firms concentrate almost exclusively on investment advice for unit trusts, requiring a mininum portfolio size and charging a fee; others will cover a wide range of investment products and charge no fees, living solely on commission. Some operate discretionary services, others do not.

They will not, however, normally offer advice about individual stocks and shares and in the majority of cases it is unlikely that they would undertake extremely sophisticated tax planning packages on their own (but then the people who require these will probably have an accountant and solicitor looking after their affairs as well).

It is important to emphasise that, at the moment, membership of FIMBRA is not a guarantee that if things go wrong, or the adviser turns out to be fraudulent, FIMBRA will pick up the bill. There will eventually be a compensation scheme covering the whole industry, but there is none at present. It is still a case of let the buyer beware.

INSURANCE BROKERS

Insurance broking does not cover simply motor and household insurance; life assurance is another area of theirs and this includes the investment-orientated products outlined in Chapter 11 and the subject of pensions as well. Many independent firms of advisers are both members of FIMBRA and registered insurance brokers – and from 1988 will be obliged to join FIMBRA if they are offering investment advice.

To this cast list must be added the clearing banks, who all offer their customers various types of advisory service; the life assurance companies themselves, many of whom have their own 'field force' of salesmen or agents, who are selling their own company's products, and the unit trust companies, of whom a number are offering unit trust advisory services, sometimes limited to their own range of trusts, and sometimes encompassing other groups as well, and finally the building societies, some of which have plans for greatly extending their range of financial advice.

HOW TO CHOOSE YOUR ADVISER

It is more likely that you will end up with an adviser most suited to your needs and preferences if you are clear about what they are. Do you, for example, want someone else to have discretion to change your holdings? Are you willing to pay a fee? Do you want tax planning advice as well as investment management – and would you prefer both from the same source?

DISCRETIONARY VERSUS NON-DISCRETIONARY SERVICES

Discretionary services probably work better, for two reasons. Firstly, your adviser is not wasting his time by contacting you every time he feels a change should be made (and possibly having to take time to explain the reasons for it). Secondly, particularly in the case of shares, though also with unit trusts, prices may move quickly, and you may lose out if you delay your decision.

Against this is the very real problem of how to know whether to trust your adviser: discretion after all, does mean you are handing over control to someone else. And while you may (indeed, ought to) be confident that he is trustworthy in the sense that he will not run off with your money, you will not necessarily know his style of management, which may be too active – he may take too many risks for your liking. In many cases, there is a simple solution to this problem: where services offer a choice, you can start off with the non-discretionary service until you have got the measure of your adviser, and then (assuming you are happy with it) move over to a discretionary service.

COMMISSION VERSUS FEES

Advisers can get twitchy when journalists start talking about commission; they feel they are being unfairly singled out and made to look like crooks. However, there is a problem here, which is simply that rewarding an adviser by means of paying him commission on the products he sells is not the best way of going about things. It may well be, in certain circumstances, that the best advice is 'do nothing' or 'buy National Savings Certificates' – but the person who advised that would be doing himself out of any reward.

Moves are afoot to make disclosure of commissions earned obligatory for some advisers – but this in my view is something of a red herring. It will not enable individuals to judge whether the advice given is impartial; it could deter people from doing things they ought to be doing (for example, starting a pension plan). The level of commission *in itself* does not reveal whether the product is good value for money or not: for that, one would have to know the level of overall charges, and since at present the rules will not be applied to all those who sell financial products, it can only complicate the issue. It now appears that commission will have to be disclosed by all 'independent' intermediaries though not by life company salesmen.

It is often said that the public are unwilling to pay realistic fees for financial advice (of course, they do – but it is usually hidden in an overall charging structure). But unless they become willing, this problem will never really be solved. In the meantime, the public continue to expect advice that is free, honest, competent and totally impartial. The surprise is that for much (though not all) of the time, they get it.

HOW TO COMPLAIN – AND WHEN NOT TO

The legal framework for investor protection has been completely overhauled and the Financial Services Act 1987 is the result. The new 'self regulatory' system, with a bunch of five self regulatory organisations (SROs) working under the direction of the Securities and Investments Board (SIB) has been described in some detail in Chapter One.

In future, if you feel the advice you received was not up to scratch, or something else has gone wrong in your dealings with a financial company, the first port of call should be the appropriate SRO. Investors are likely to come across just two of the five SROs: FIMBRA, the SRO for financial intermediaries, and TSA – The Securities Association, representing members of the Stock Exchange. Then there is LAUTRO (the Life and Unit Trust Regulatory Organisation); this would be the port of call if you wanted to complain about a product's advertising, for example, or the conduct of a life company's salesman, and IMRO, the Investment Managers Regulatory Organisation. The last of the five, the Association of Futures Brokers and Dealers (AFBD) is unlikely to have much relevance for private investors.

SIB is insistent that each SRO has a proper complaints procedure with access to an independent 'ombudsman' or referee to hear cases of complaint. At the time of writing, the SROs are still finalising their procedures and scurrying around trying to set systems up. Remember, the new system is not due to become effective till early in 1988 though both FIMBRA and the Stock Exchange have established complaints procedures in place.

In the meantime, there are three independent ombudsmen who have been established for some time: the Insurance Ombudsman, the Banking Ombudsman and the Building Societies Ombudsman.

The Insurance Ombudsman has been running the longest, having been set up in 1981. His field of reference includes household and motor insurance and life insurance. Around 70 companies belong to the scheme, and if you have a policy with one of these groups and feel you have a legitimate cause of complaint, then this is the place to go.

All three Ombudsmen publish leaflets on their services, available from the addresses noted below. It's important to realise that the powers of the Ombudsmen are limited: the Banking Ombudsman, for example, won't get involved if your bank manager has turned you down for a loan. All three also require that you take your complaint up to the highest level within the company concerned first, before knocking on their doors.

These Ombudsmen will still be operating next year, and there are going to be situations where an individual simply won't know which of the various avenues open to him he should use for his complaint. The Consumer's Association has recommended that there should be a sort of clearing house for complaints, with a single, well-publicised address. Whether this will happen or not remains to be seen. In the meantime, a recent paperback called *The Abbey Financial Rights Handbook* by Wendy Elkington, published by Rosters Limited, set out the current situation clearly.

DO YOU NEED ADVICE?

This chapter has assumed that you will be looking for an outside source of advice – but of course, there is no reason why you should not manage your own affairs, although if you wish to deal in shares you are obliged to go via an intermediary (the stockbroker).

Financial Intermediaries, Managers and Brokers Regulatory Association, 22 Great Tower Street, London EC3R 5AQ

The Insurance Ombudsman, 31 Southampton Row, London WC1B 5HY
01-242 8613

The Building Societies Ombudsman, Rooms 11 to 16, First Floor, Grosvenor Gardens House, 35–37 Grosvenor Gardens, London SW1X 7AW
01-931 0044

The Banking Ombudsman, Citadel House, 5-11 Fetter Lane, London EC4 A1BR
01-583 1395

The Stock Exchange and The Securities Association, Old Broad Street, London EC2N 1HP
01-588 2355

CHAPTER 13

FINANCIAL PLANNING IN PRACTICE: MODEL PORTFOLIOS

If financial planning is not an art, it is certainly a very inexact science, for at least two reasons: the 'best' investments (in the most meaningful sense of the word) are those that go up the highest – and there is no way of finding out what these are in advance! The second reason is that financial planning is about people, rather than some computer-designed construction called 'the investor'.

The following examples are all misleading in a sense, in that few of us are in a position where we have, say, precisely £10,000 or £30,000 to invest, and a completely clean slate as far as investment are concerned. Most of us will have acquired something along the way – a building society account, some inherited shares maybe, or we will have built up pension entitlements in our jobs or taken out an endowment mortgage with the prospect of a surplus at the end of the mortgage term.

Many advisers will send out lengthy questionnaires on your current financial situation before they will even begin to advise you, and the following are fairly brief sketches of what are hopefully 'typical' investors, but with all the shortcomings that that implies.

The first two of these ages taken here are split into two sections. They deal with slightly different problems, but the basic difference is that the first is for people who are fairly averse to risk taking, the second for those who view some risk taking with equanimity. The oldest age has one section only, as the investments should, anyway, be pretty much on the cautious side and the choice will depend largely on the level of income required.

The out and out speculator is not catered for in these pages – not because he is disapproved of, but because he is likely to be investing on a much more active basis; going for short-term rewards. Suggesting a 'model' portfolio for him is something that only a stockbroker can do, at a particular point in time.

The portfolios below are not intended to hold good for ever and ever; both your circumstances and the outside world will change, meaning regular reviews are necessary. They are meant to be a long term 'skeleton' to be fleshed out with suitable investment advice at the appropriate time.

Finally, all the investors here are assumed to be male – for no very good reason. They could just as well be women.

PORTFOLIO NUMBER ONE

A man and wife in their early thirties have partly inherited, partly accumulated, a lump sum of £10,000. They have one small child, and a house they are buying by means of an endowment mortgage. The husband is a basic rate taxpayer and a member of his company's pension scheme. At present he intends remaining with his company throughout his career. His wife is not working. They have more or less sufficient income for their needs and do not want to spend any of their investment. They might consider moving house in about five years' time, but this is the only vague plan they have. They do not like taking risks very much and would probably have kept all their money in a building society, were it not for the fact that the unexpected inheritance has made them a little more adventurous.

Suggested portfolio	£	Comments
Building society account	2,000	Emergency kitty – seven-day notice account for higher interest.
Friendly society plan linked to building society	2,000	Lump sum investment into plan: long term (ten years); safe, and tax efficient. One plan for husband and wife.
Guaranteed Growth bond	2,000	Another fixed interest investment, but this time with fixed rates, offering protection if interest rates fall. Five year investment. Could help with house moving expenses.
UK General unit trust	2,000	Giving some exposure to equities medium to long term investment.
US (or International) unit trust	2,000	Widely spread, so less risk than direct shareholdings. Should be less volatile than specialist trusts. Choose accumulation units if no income required.

PORTFOLIO NUMBER TWO

The same basic situation as number one, but happy to take some risks. The husbands also considers that he could well become liable to higher rate tax in the next year or so.

FINANCIAL PLANNING IN PRACTICE: MODEL PORTFOLIOS

Suggested portfolio	£	Comments
Building society	2,000	Emergency kitty.
Friendly society plan, invested 50% in equities	1,000	Lump sum investment into plan: ten year investment. Tax efficient.
Unit trust portfolio total 7,000 as follows:		How this is divided will depend (a) on conditions when he invests and (b) on how actively he wants to monitor it.
UK Growth or Recovery trust	3,000	Could well follow suggestions on left: the first three give a good spread; the Hong Kong/commodity/technology element is for speculation and possible high rewards. An alternative would be to take out a Personal Equity Plan for £2,400, and adjust the unit trust portfolio accordingly.
US Growth trust	1,000	
Japan Growth trust	1,000	
European trust	1,000	
Specialist trust – e.g. Hong Kong or Commodities or Technology	1,000	

General comments, numbers one and two

These portfolios have not mentioned two important subjects in financial planning, pensions or life assurance. Adequate life assurance is extremely important and should be the first thing to think about before investment. As far as pensions are concerned, if the individual was self-employed, he should probably already be putting savings into a pension plan. If he is a member of a pension scheme, it is probably too soon to think about anything extra he might do along these lines – he could well change jobs between now and retirement which could put out any planning done now.

PORTFOLIO NUMBER THREE

A couple in their mid-forties have inherited a sizeable sum and want to invest £30,000. They are buying their own house and living within their income, but would welcome a bit more spending money. They have no plans to move house. The husband is a civil servant and can expect to retire on an index-linked pension of half his salary at 60. They are conservative investors, and but for the unwelcome realisation that they would become liable to higher rate tax if they invested the entire sum in bank deposits and building societies, would probably have done so.

Suggested portfolio	£	Comments
Building society	3,000	Emergency kitty.
Friendly society plan, linked to building societies	2,000	Long term investment (ten years) safe and tax efficient. One plan each.

Suggested portfolio	£	Comments
National Savings Certificates	5,000	Fixed rate, 5 year term; returns are tax-free. Protected against subsequent falls in interest rates, though not against future rises.
Index-linked gilt, e.g. 'Tsy 2½% 2001'	3,000	The ultimate 'safe' investment, chosen for its maturity date, i.e. around the time he retires (at which point a re-think will be necessary).
Medium-coupon gilt, e.g. 'Tsy 9½% 1999'	3,000	Again, chosen for maturity date, near retirement. Will provide some income now, though a small loss on maturity. Many other possibilities here: should consult a broker.
Managed bond	4,000	Well spread, asset-backed investment. Can withdraw 5 per cent a year tax-free for 20 years or leave to accumulate if income not needed.
International income unit trust	2,000	Giving international exposure; less risk than growth trust. Some income now, also prospects of capital appreciation.
Portfolio of 'blue chip' shares – or UK General or Income unit trusts, or investment trusts. Use Personal Equity Plan for first £2,400	8,000	More asset-backed investment – but still leaves overall portfolio over 50 per cent in fixed interest investments. Given his age (i.e. plenty of time until retirement) this should be ample, even for conservative investor.

PORTFOLIO NUMBER FOUR

Again, a couple in their forties who have a lump sum of £30,000 to invest. The husband is self-employed and a higher rate taxpayer. He is used to taking risks and wants his money to 'work for him'. No immediate needs for cash or income, but will have to consider his pension prospects.

Suggested portfolio	£	Comments
Building society	1,000	Small emergency kitty; can always 'borrow' from the sums he has put aside for tax if short-term problems arise.
Pension plan	5,000	Using the 'catch up' provisions to top-up previous premiums paid to maximum allowed. Uses single premium plans and splits between with-profits and unit-linked. Will cut his next tax bill by £2000+.
Investment trust shares	5,000	Split between one international trust and one specialist Far Eastern trust.

Suggested portfolio	£	Comments
Business Expansion Scheme	3,000	Speculative but will reduce his tax bill, and could provide high rewards. A BES fund will spread his investment, therefore slightly less risk of losing the lot.
International unit trusts, specialist funds, e.g. European, Far Eastern, American Recovery	6,000	More international exposure, best obtained through unit trusts or investor investment trusts. Intends to monitor actively.
UK equities – held direct or UK Smaller Company and Recovery unit trusts or a portfolio of investment trusts.	10,000	Emphasis on growth stocks; may include some USM companies. Could put some in specialist unit trusts. Should use a Personal Equity Plan up to £2,400.

PORTFOLIO NUMBER FIVE

A 55-year-old has a lump sun of £35,000 to invest – partly inherited, partly accumulated, partly the proceeds from an endowment policy, which has just matured. He is a member of his company's pension scheme, but will retire at 65 on less than half his salary, thanks to job changes in the past. He is a basic rate taxpayer, and has no need for extra income at this stage. He does not like taking risks and feels, anyway, that it would be inappropriate to do so given his circumstances.

Suggested portfolio	£	Comments
Building society	4,000	Emergency kitty.
Friendly society plan, linked to building societies	2,000	Lump sum investment into 10 year plans: safe, tax efficient, and will mature at time he retires.
Temporary annuity to fund regular payments into Additional Voluntary Contributions Scheme (AVC)	7,000	Best way of increasing his pension prospects. The annuity should provide income of around £1,000 a year to put into AVCs, which must be kept up on regular basis. Will receive tax relief on his contributions.
Managed bonds	8,000	Well spread asset-backed investment. Can start withdrawing 10 per cent of original investment tax-free from age of 65 if wishes, for following 10 years.
Index-linked gilts	4,000	To provide guaranteed protection against inflation – could chose a gilt maturing near the time he retires.
Income unit trusts	10,000	These will provide a low but rising income. Can re-invest income if not needed at present.

PORTFOLIO NUMBER SIX

A newly-retired couple who have a lump sum to invest, primarily with a view to producing an income.

Option 1: high income now, but no growth
Non-taxpayers: National Savings Income Bond; high coupon gilts; local authority loans.
Basic rate taxpayers: building society long term notice account, high interest bank account, guaranteed income bond.
Higher rate taxpayers: including those caught in the 'age allowance trap' (for incomes between £9,400 and £10,675, where the extra allowance is progressively withdrawn, giving an effective marginal rate of 50 per cent): guaranteed income bonds, offshore sterling 'roll up' fund, building society and bank deposits.

Option 2: medium income now, some growth
Non-taxpayers: high income unit trusts (and reclaim tax paid on income) combined with, for example, National Savings Income Bond.
Basic rate taxpayers: High income unit trusts, 'back to back' income plan.
Higher rate taxpayers: income unit trust, possibly managed fund; withdrawing 5 per cent a year tax-free (especially if expects to become basic rate taxpayer in future).

Option 3: low income now, good prospects for growth
Non taxpayer: income unit trusts, reclaiming tax paid.
Basic rate taxpayers: income unit trusts.
Higher rate taxpayers: income unit trusts and portfolio of growth trusts (consider encashing units on a regular basis to use tax-free capital gains as 'income').

Option 4: high income at any cost
Consider taking out an annuity. May, however, be preferable to wait a few more years, as annuity rates rise sharply from age 65 onwards. Remember no capital is returned on death.

INDEX

Accountants
   financial advice, 13, 14, 145
   Recognised Professional Bodies, 13
Age allowance trap, 157
   guaranteed income and growth bonds, 36
   offshore money funds, 39
Annuities, life assurance companies, 115, 120-2
Antiques, 131
Art objects, 131
Association of Futures Brokers and Dealers (AFBD), 13, 149

Back to back income plans 115, 122-3
Banking Act (1987), 30
Banks, 32
   buying and selling shares, 60
   collapse, 3
   current account, 21-2
   deposit accounts, 23
   financial advice, 141, 142-4
   high interest accounts, 23
   high interest cheque accounts, 22
   interest rates, 20
   legal protection of deposits, 30
   merchant, 22, 141, 143-4
   money funds, 22
   offshore, 3, 24
   Ombudsman, 149-50
   polarisation, 15
   tax deducted at source, 19
   term deposit accounts, 23-4
Bear market, 71
Benefit societies, 123-4
Big Bang, 12, 51-2
Blue chips, 71
Bonds *see* Guaranteed income and growth bonds; Life assurance investments; Local authority securities
Broker *see* Stockbroker
Building societies, 22, 32
   Compounded Annual Rate, 25
   deposit accounts, 24, 25
   financial advice, 15, 143
   legal protection of deposits, 30
   Ombudsman, 149-50
   share accounts, 24-5
   tax deducted at source, 19
   unit trust performance compared, 96
Building Societies Act (1976), 15
Bull market, 71
Business Expansion Scheme (BES), 137-8

Capital Gains Tax (CGT), 6-7
   annual exemption, 6
   friendly societies, 124
   gilt-edged securities 44-5
   indexation allowance, 6
   investment trusts, 105
   life assurance investments, 7, 117, 118, 120-1
   major exemptions, 6-7
   offshore funds, 88, 103
   roll-up funds, 38, 103
   traded options, 70
   unit trust, 81, 83
Capital Transfer Tax (CTT) *see* Inheritance Tax
Carpets, investing in, 136
Charges, 11, 12, 39, 50, 52, 62-3, 77-9, 107-8, 144-6, 148
Charitable donations, 7
Commission, 12, 50, 52, 61-2, 145, 148
Commodity funds, offshore, 103
Composite Rate Tax (CRT), 19-20
Contango, 71
Convertibles, 70-1
Coupon, meaning, 42
Credit cards, 21

Death
   guaranteed income and growth bonds, 35
   life assurance annuities, 121-2
Debentures, 71
Decorations for gallantry, 7
Diamonds, 11, 131, 134-5
Dividends, 57-9
   cover, 58-9
   final, 57
   income tax, 6
   interim, 57
   judging, 57-8
   price sensitive information, 58
   yield, 58
Dealing costs 52, 62-3

Equities, 9, 51-73
   buying and selling, 60-3
   company general meetings, 56
   company liquidation, 56
   dealing costs, 52, 62-3
   dividends, 57-9
   exercise price, 68-9
   foreign, 51
   fully paid, 56
   futures contract, 68
   gambling on, 70
   gilts compared, 47
   indices, 63-4
   insider dealing, 58

158 INDEX

investment risks, 3
limit orders, 61
limited liability, 51, 56
long term growth records, 16
"no frills" dealing service, 61, 144
options, 68-70
ordinary shares, 55-6
overseas investments, 10
partly paid, 56
Personal Equity Plans, 72-3
place in portfolio, 64-8
price moves, 56-7, 105-6
price/earnings ratio, 59-60
private investor, 54-5
reverse yield gap, 58
share shops, 61
spread of risk, 10
unit trust investments, 76
yield gap, 58

Fees, 61, 148
Financial advisers, 145-50
    polarisation, 13, 15
Financial Intermediaries, Managers and Brokers Regulatory Association (FIMBRA), 13, 146, 147, 149
Financial Services Act (1987), 12-13, 142, 148
Foreign currency
    managed currency fund, 37, 102
    offshore fund, 37-8, 102-3
Foreign shares, 51
Forestry, investing in, 136
Franked and unfranked income, 117
Fraud, SIB compensation-scheme, 13
Friendly societies, 123-4
FT-Actuaries Indices, 3, 4, 59
FT-All Share Index, 63-4, 66
FT-Industrial Ordinary Index (FT-30), 63-4
FT-Stock Exchange Index (FT-SE 100), 63-4, 68
Futures
    contract, 68
    gold, 134

Gambling and betting
    on shares, 70
    winnings, 7
Gifts with reservation, 8-9
Gilt-edged securities, 9, 41-51
    bought through Post Office, 44, 46, 49
    break-even inflation rate, 48-9
    British Gas, 42
    British Transport, 42
    buying and selling, 49-50
    commission, 50
    "coupon", 42, 43, 45, 46
    dealing in, 9
    descriptive terms, 42-4
    equities compared, 47
    Exchequer, 42
    factors affecting prices, 41-2
    fixed rate, 48

gilt unit trust, 50
gross redemption yield, 43
held to redemption, 20
index-linked, 5, 44, 48, 48-9
long term growth records, 16
National Savings Stock Register, 49
negotiable securities, 41
net redemption yield, 45, 50
payment of interest, 45-6
price quotation, 42-3
private investors, 46-7
redemption dates, 43, 46
short-, medium- and long-dated, 43, 46
single premium life assurance bond, 50
stockbrokers, 48, 49, 50
tax position, 7, 44-5, 46
Treasury, 42
undated, 43-4, 46
unit trust investments, 76
War Loans, 42, 44
Gold, 11, 131, 133-4
Granny bonds, 29
Growth bonds *see* Guaranteed income and growth bonds
Guaranteed income and growth bonds, 20, 34-7, 39
    age allowance trap, 36
    death of bondholder, 35
    legal protection, 36
    offshore, 36-7
    single life basis, 35-6
    tax position, 36-7

Income tax, 6
    composite rate, 19-20
    deducted at source, 19
    gilt-edged securities, 44, 46
    guaranteed income and growth bonds, 36-7
    higher rate payers, 19-20, 36, 113, 133
    investment trusts, 105
    life assurance investments, 117, 120-1
    National Savings Certificates, 26-8
    personal allowances, 7
    rates, 7
    unit trusts, 81, 83
Index-linked
    certificates, 29
    gilt-edged securities, 44, 48-9
Inflation, 3-5
    break-even inflation rate, 48-9
    gilt-edged securities, 5, 41
    indexation allowance, 6
    tangible investments, 133
Inheritance Tax, 7-9, 145
    gifts with reservation, 8-9
    lifetime gifts, 8
Insider dealing, 58
Insurance
    brokers, 141, 146-7
    Ombudsman, 149-50
    see also Life assurance investments
Interest
    Compounded Annual Rate (CAR), 25

INDEX

fixed, 9, 20-1, 25
variable, 20
Investment Managers Regulatory Organisation (IMRO), 13, 149
Investment trusts, 51, 105-14
bid and offer prices, 106
characteristics, 108-9
charges, 107-8
gearing, 107, 108, 110
international outlook, 109
investment categories, 109
limited life trusts, 110
publication of prices, 109-10
risk spreading, 105
share price discount, 105-7, 110
share price performance, 112
split capital trusts, 110-11
stockbrokers, 114
taxation, 105
unit trusts compared, 106, 108
warrants, 113-14
Investments
fixed capital, 19-39
overseas, 10
pensions *see* Pensions
risks involved, 2-3, 10

Jewellery, 135
Jobbers *see* Market makers

Legal protection, 30, 36, 148-50
Licensed deposit-takers, 22
Life assurance investments, 115-23, 145
annuities, 115, 120-2
back to back income plans, 115, 122-3
broker bonds, 119-20
capital gains tax, 7
guaranteed income and growth bonds, 34-7
managed funds, 116
offshore, 36-7
personalised bonds, 119
property funds, 116
risk spreading, 115
single premium bonds, 50, 115-19
taxation, 117, 118, 120-1
unit trusts compared, 118-19
Life Assurance and Unit Trust Regulatory Organisation (LAUTRO), 13, 149
Limited liability, 51
Limited life trusts, 110
Lloyd's, membership of, 138-9
Loans
Bureau, 33-4
local authority, 33-4
Local authority securities
default, 33
mortgage bonds, 33
negotiable bonds, 33-4
London International Financial Futures Exchange LIFFE, 68
Loss
capital, 3

foreign currency funds, 37

Managed currency fund, 37
Market makers, 52
commission, 12
Mortgage bonds, local authority, 33

National Insurance contributions rebate, 126
National Savings, 19, 32, 41
Certificates, 5, 7, 20, 26-9, 30-1
deposit bonds, 26, 30-1
Government guarantee, 32
guide to, 30-1
income bonds, 25-6, 30-1
investment account, 26, 30-1
ordinary account, 26, 30-1
Stock Register, 49
Negotiable securities, 33, 41

Offshore
banks, 24
gold investments, 133, 134
life assurance companies, 36-7
share pushing companies, 54
Offshore funds, 37-9, 75
accumulator status, 38, 87-8, 103
age allowance trap, 39
commodity funds, 103
disadvantages, 88-9
distributor status, 38, 87, 89, 103
flexibility, 87
foreign currency, 37-8, 102-3
investment choices, 102-3
management fee, 39
minimum investment, 39
sterling fund, 37-8, 102-3
tax treatment, 38-9, 87-8
umbrella, 89, 118
Over the Counter stocks (OTC), 71
Overseas, investments, 10

Paintings, 131
Pensions, 11, 125-30, 145
Additional Voluntary Contribution (AVC), 127-8
final salary, 125-6, 128
money purchase, 125, 126-7
National Insurance rebates, 126
opting out of company scheme, 125
personal pension plan, 126, 128-9
State Earnings Related Pension Scheme (SERPS), 125, 127
taxation, 125
Personal Equity Plans (PEPs), 72-3
Platinum, 131, 134
Policyholders Protection Act, 36
Pooled investment *see* Investment trust; Unit trust
Pools, capital gains tax exemption, 7
Portfolios, model, 151-7
Preference shares, 70, 76
Premium Bonds, 7, 28-9, 30-1
Price/earnings ratio (p/e), 59-60

INDEX

Privatisation, 54-5
Property
  capital gains tax exemption, 7
  funds, 116

Retail Price Index (RPI), 41
Reverse yield gap, 58
Risk spreading, 2-3, 75
  investment trusts, 105
  life assurance investments, 115
Roll-up fund, 37-9, 88, 103
Rule 163(2) company, 71

School fees, 11, 145
Securities and Investments Board (SIB), 12-13, 142, 146, 149
Share pushing companies, 54
Share shop, 61
Shareholders, 55
Shares *see* Equities; Gilt-edged securities
Smaller companies trust, 100, 108
Solicitors as financial advisers, 13
Split capital trusts, 110-11, 113
Spouse
  gifts between, 8
  guaranteed income and growth bonds, 35-6
  life assurance annuities, 121-2
Stag, 71-2
Sterling offshore fund, 37-8, 102-3
Stock Exchange, 9, 10, 51
  "Big Bang", 12, 51-2
  listed companies, 56
  private investor, 54-5
Stock market terms, 71-2
Stockbrokers, 52, 141, 144-5
  buying and selling shares, 60-2
  commission, 12, 50, 52, 61-2, 145
  gilt-edged securities, 46, 49, 50
  instructing, 62-3
  investment trusts, 114

Tangible investments, 131-6
  artistic value, 131
  buying and selling margins, 133
  collectable items, 131-2
  ephemera, 132
  insurance and storage costs, 133
  intrinsic value, 131, 133-5
  useable items, 132-3
Tax
  Business Expansion Scheme, 138
  certificate of tax deposit, 37, 39
  composite rate, 19-20
  friendly societies, 123-4
  future tax bills, 37
  gilt-edged securities, 44-5
  investment trusts, 105
  life assurance, 117, 118, 120-1
  offshore funds, 38-9, 87-8
  pensions, 125
  reclaiming, 44
  see also Capital Gains Tax; Income Tax; Inheritance Tax; Value Added Tax

Technology trust, 100, 108
The Securities Association (TSA), 13, 149
Theatre productions, investing in, 136-7
Third Market, 53
Traded options, 68-70

Umbrella funds, 89, 118
Unit trusts, 51, 75-86, 91-104
  accumulation units, 81
  adding to holding, 84
  bid and offer prices, 79-81
  building society performance compared, 96
  buying and selling, 86
  capital growth orientated, 81, 91, 99-102
  charges, 77-9
  commodity and energy shares, 93
  distribution or income units, 81
  equalisation payment, 81
  exempt trusts, 94
  financial and property shares, 93
  fund of funds, 82-3
  general, 98-9
  gilt, 50
  gilt and fixed interest growth, 92-3
  gilt and fixed interest income, 92
  income from, 81, 91, 95-7
  international, 93
  international income, 93
  investment trust units, 93
  investment trusts compared, 106, 108
  life assurance bonds compared, 118-19
  managed funds, 82-3, 93-4
  mixed income, 92
  overseas income trusts, 91-2, 98, 100
  recovery trusts, 100
  regular income schemes, 84-5, 98
  regular savings schemes, 84
  regulation, 76-7
  risk spreading, 75, 77
  share exchange schemes, 83
  smaller companies trusts, 100, 108
  special situations trusts, 100
  switching trusts, 78-9
  taxation of, 81, 83
  technology trusts, 100, 108
  UK equity income, 92
  UK general, 92
  UK growth, 92
  withdrawal schemes, 85
Unlisted Securities Market (USM), 53-4, 72, 76

Value Added Tax, coins, 133

War Loan, 42, 44
Wine, investing in, 135

Yearlings, 33
Yield gap, 58